# ⇛ T H E   E R R A T I C S

THE Erratics

VICKI LAVEAU-HARVIE

*Alfred A. Knopf*
*New York*
*2020*

Library of Congress Cataloging-in-Publication Data
Names: Laveau-Harvie, Vicki, author.
Title: The erratics / Vicki Laveau-Harvie.
Description: First edition. | New York : Alfred A. Knopf, 2020.
Identifiers: LCCN 2019045789 | ISBN 9780525658610 (hardcover) |
    ISBN 9780525658627 (ebook)
Subjects: LCSH: Laveau-Harvie, Vicki. | Mothers and daughters—
    Biography. | Dysfunctional families—Biography. | Mothers—Mental
    health—Biography. | Abused husbands—Biography.
Classification: LCC HQ755.86.L38 2020 | DDC 306.87—dc23
LC record available at https://lccn.loc.gov/2019045789

*For my children and my grandchildren*

※

Tens of thousands of years ago, the Cordilleran Ice Sheet snaked down the east side of the Alaskan Rocky Mountains, through what is now the province of Alberta in Canada, and into the U.S. state of Montana. As it moved, it deposited gigantic rocks called erratics along its path. These form what is known as the Foothills Erratics Train.

One of those huge boulders sits in a landscape of uncommon beauty a few miles from the Canadian town of Okotoks. The town takes its name from the Blackfoot word for the rock, "Okatok."

Countless years ago, the Okotoks Erratic broke in two and became unsafe to climb upon. A Blackfoot legend recounts that it fractured as it thundered across the landscape in pursuit of Napi, the Blackfoot trickster character. He had rested on the rock and left his cloak as an offering of thanks, but when it began to rain, he took it back. Furious, the rock chased after him. None of his animal friends could stop it, until finally the bats broke it in two along a fault line and saved him.

The Erratic dominates the landscape, roped off and isolated, the danger it presents to anyone trespassing palpable and documented on the signs posted around it.

※

# ⇒ THE ERRATICS

M y sister unhooks the chart from the foot of my mother's bed and reads.

My mother is not in the bed. My sister takes her pen, which is always to hand, around her neck or poked into a pocket and, with the air of entitlement of a medical professional, writes "MMA" in large letters at the bottom of the chart.

MMA.

Mad as a meat-ax.

My sister learned this expression from me yesterday. She has latched on to it like a child wresting a toy from another.

We have come to visit my mother, in rehab for a broken hip in this prairie hospital, a place that could be far worse than it is. It is set down here, plain and brown, on flat farmland, but the foothills start rolling westward just outside town and you see them from the windows. They roll on, smooth, rhythmic, and comforting, until they bump into the stern and inscrutable face of the Rockies eighty miles thataway.

In summer the fields are sensible, right-angled squares of sulfur-yellow and clean, pale green, rapeseed and young wheat. In winter the cold will kill you. Nothing personal. Your lungs will freeze as Christmas lights tracing the outlines of white frame houses wink cheerfully through air so clear and hard it shatters.

MMA, I say. They won't know what that means. You don't say that here in Southern Alberta, even in urban centers. It's a down-underism, an antipodeanism. Maybe they'll see that on the chart and give her some medication called MMA and kill her.

Do we care? my sister asks. She hangs the chart back on the foot of the bed as my mother wheels into the room, gaunt, her favorite look, with a black fringe and bobbed hair. Hats off for carrying that off at ninety. Her sinewy hands coerce the wheels of her chair forward faster than you are supposed to go if you need this chair.

She is wearing a hospital gown and a pair of fuchsia boxer shorts. Not hers. Obviously not hers.

She remarks that it is strange that she cannot have her own things to wear, that she must wear this strange outfit. We don't think to question. We believe in strange. We believe whatever. There's no other way to go at this.

We have run the nurses' station gauntlet to get to her. We have announced ourselves at the counter as her daughters, on our first visit to this rehab ward. We are her daughters, we say, when challenged about why we are in this corridor.

No, you're not, the nurse says, not even looking up from her papers.

But we are. We're sure.

No, she insists. She only had one daughter and she died a long time ago. Now she has none.

My sister cries out from the heart, startling me. Look at me, she cries. Do I look dead?

I don't think she is looking too good, but there is something more pressing. Why, I ask her, are you the daughter who gets to exist? Even if you're dead now. Not to put too fine a point on it but if anyone should get to be dead, it's me. I was born first.

The physio strolling by stops to ask who we are and what the matter is. We stare at her, wanting to say all that is the matter, wanting to unroll the whole carpet of what is the matter and smooth it out, drawing attention to the motifs, combing the fringed edges into some order, vacuuming the patterned surface until clarity emerges. We wonder how to begin.

They are saying, the nurse tells the physio, that they're the duchess's daughters. But she has no children.

You've got it wrong, the physio says. Little bird of a person, you'd never know it of her, but she had eighteen kids. Imagine, eighteen. And only one boy. Heartbroken she was. Told me herself. In tears. Oh, she had kids all right. Nobody around when you need them though.

I draw breath. I can work with this. See, I say to the nurse, there you go. We can't speak for the others, but we'd like to see her.

※

Just in case we're having too much fun with this, let's go back a notch in time. Only a little while, don't be afraid, not far enough to get caught in the starry wheeling vertigo of the slow-mo free-fall no-up-and-no-down that is the more distant past. We will go there—chronology has its uses—but not just yet.

Some weeks earlier then. The beginning of winter.

When winter comes, summer is the memory that keeps people going, the remembrance of the long slanting dusk, peonies massed along the path, blossoms as big as balloons, crimson satin petals deepening to the black of dried blood in the waning light, deer on the lawns, stock-still. Some people here, not transplants from the city like my parents, still make preserves in the summer, crab apple jelly, tomato chutney, apple butter. They keep the jars safe through the autumn months, when the hay is rolled and the young coyotes practice yipping at the moon from the edge of the stubbled fields, to eat from when the snow flies.

My parents live in paradise, twenty acres with a ranch house on a rise, nothing between you and the sky and the distant mountains. Overlapping cedar shingles on the roof that will last for generations or until the house falls down.

No near neighbors.

The house is paradise in the same way the Hotel California is: a fortress with many bedrooms, a wine cellar, a mud room, a huge windowless library, a grand piano in the great room, two furnaces, and a bomb shelter dug five meters deep into the hill in case Cuban missiles are ever aimed at the Turner Valley oilfields or the trout in Sheep Creek.

The doors of this house open to no one. The phone rings unanswered, unheard by my father, who finds his life livable if he takes the batteries out of his hearing aid, and ignored by my mother, who knows the world is out to get her. The leaves of the trembling aspens can shake all day like gold coins in air as clear as cider, but this is not a welcoming place.

So, early winter in the house a mile from the six-lane highway running straight south to the States. On this day a solid ribbon of eighteen-wheelers is gunning it full throttle for Great Falls, Montana, or Boise, Idaho, making the most of the open roads and hardly believing their luck, just a drift of powder across the road when you gear up, like icing sugar from a doughnut.

In the kitchen, my mother's hipbone crumbles and breaks and she falls.

They must have phoned someone. They must have opened the door to strangers who came to help. These strangers will have walked into this time-capsule house sealed against the outside world for a decade. The breaching of the no-go zone must have made a sound like a crowbar splintering wood.

Some days later, at the hospital, I prop myself up in a midblue tub chair in the social worker's room. Outside the sky is colorless, the landscape dun and dry, a wasteland waiting for snow.

The year's work is done on the land, and the wards on the floor below my mother's are full of farmers and ranchers under observation for a vague and undefinable malaise. It's the same every year. I blame the landscape, out there pining like a suitorless spinster for the snow, for the blinding swathe of white that will mask its disgrace and wrap it in beauty until the spring when, against all odds, bountiful things will pierce the earth, grow and flower.

At my parents' house, where I stay with my sister, my stick-figure skin-and-bones father creeps along the hallway at night to turn the thermostats up on the furnaces. My sister sighs and mutters as she turns them down and slams the door to her bedroom.

I don't care either way. I just wish she wouldn't sleep

with her window wide open. Hasn't she read *In Cold Blood*? These sparsely populated spaces where the buffalo no longer roam draw sociopaths, people with guns and opportunistic local crackheads.

We are no match for any of those, such as we are: two women well past any semblance of bloom, often mistaken for twins in supermarkets and gas stations, which pisses off the younger of the two, and a shaking, shambling old man who is not, as I first feared, terminally stricken. It is simpler than that. He has been starving for some time and suffers, like Patty Hearst before him, from Stockholm syndrome.

So I sit in my tub chair facing the young social worker dispatched to get a bead on us, and we are broaching the subject of my mother, her fractiousness which is disrupting hospital routine, her dicey rehab prospects, and her eventual discharge.

Or at least my vis-à-vis is trying to broach. I am gamely trying to pretend that I do not see her flipping through the index pages of the *Family Justice and Equity Handbook* in her mind, looking for an appropriate heading. My mother has told her that my sister and I disappeared decades ago and that the investigators she hired on several continents found no trace of us. But now, somehow sensing her frailty, smelling death and money, we have come in to land feet-first, like vultures in a western, wanting to put her away.

The last bit is true.

The young woman eyes me cautiously. It must have been hard when you were growing up, she begins.

I look balefully at her. I mean, she says, with a mother

so . . . Her voice dies out. She looks to the landscape for help. I want to get this over with. I help.

Extreme? I say. Mercurial? Challenging, yes. Quite a vibrant personality, my mother.

To be blunt, she says, your mother can be difficult.

So. They've noticed.

I'm ready for this. I have rehearsed with my sister for this. I have had to, because here is what happened yesterday.

Suppertime, yesterday evening. My sister is carving a chicken for dinner when the phone rings. She speaks on the phone for some minutes, carving knife in hand, then she hangs up and announces that they want to see us at the hospital to talk about my mother, in particular about something they call her difficulty adjusting. My sister looks to the ceiling and begins to exult like a true believer giving praise.

Finally, she cries. Somebody will finally believe us! They can see how crazy she is. They'll believe us now. She skewers a couple of the old nonbelievers from our childhood on her carving knife on the way back to the stove.

In a flash I see our situation clearly. It's like a split screen, a two-part problem my sister and I have not spoken about in clear terms in the hours since we arrived here.

My mother is, by virtue of a crumbling bone, an osteoporotic hip, confined exactly where we need her to be: in a hospital, for an extended period of time, away from my father. If we're smart enough, we'll use the respite this broken bone affords us to make sure she never comes home at all, that she will remain confined, not for her hip but for a completely different reason, and that my father will have room to recover from her regimen of starvation and brainwashing.

They don't care about crazy, I say. It's not about crazy. She's in there for hip rehab and she's giving them a lot of trouble. They just want to make sure that we are ready for her to be discharged as soon as they can decently do it.

Watch what you wish for, I warn her. We won't want them to believe she's always been crazy. If they believe that, we can't make a case for keeping her confined from now on, somewhere where she can't kill Dad by increments.

Or in one go, I add, thinking of the rifle in its chamois cover propped in a corner of the study downstairs.

We'll need them to believe in a slightly modified metaphor: an unstable slope that has recently given way; a slippage like the Frank Slide in the Rockies that killed scores; a sudden cascading deterioration, maybe during the anesthetic for her hip. It could be true. It happens. We need her not to come home because she will perish in this house and so will her husband, so she must be seen as unable to cope now, not as having always been that way.

This upsets my sister. She wants validation, vindication. She wants it to be about crazy. She wants to paint "I told you so" on the walls of the hospital, in blood. She has a case, but she can only indulge herself at a cost I am not willing to pay. I know I'm right.

I win. With bad grace, she rehearses with me after dinner. We stand, like airline hostesses, feet together. Here, I say, is your normal range of personality traits. I hold my hands a foot apart, waist height, palms facing, as though pressing on the ends of a wholemeal sandwich loaf.

And this, I say, spreading my arms wide as though indicating an exit on the right, we wish, and an exit on the left, if only, is my mother's range. Tendency to extremes, challenging for loved ones. "Loved" in quotation marks.

And now, just recently, this unfortunate slippage, which has pushed her beyond any parameters our arms can encompass. Eyes down, palms up, helpless.

That is what we will say.

Repeat after me.

So, back in the room with the social worker. I know she's just doing her job, trying to decide if she can believe my mother about us, to make a call about how safe my mother will be if sent home to people like us.

You must surely, she says, harbor some, like, uh . . . She gives up.

Resentment, you mean? Anger, hurt, confusion? It's a continuum. I stop short of dead-straight pain, rage, despair and homicidal acting out. She nods and nods.

I think suddenly of the pumpjacks they put on wellheads to pull the crude oil from the earth around here. My dad would take me with him sometimes, out to the oilfields on weekends, and I would watch the pumps, their heads pecking patiently at the ground like big clumsy birds,

reliable and benevolent, assuring the prosperity of all and
sundry.

No, I say, I do not feel those. She blinks. You wonder
why? I prompt, pressing my advantage. She does.

Because my mother opened doors for us, I say. I stand
up, for effect and because I have a cramp in my foot, probably DVT, and fling the door open to illustrate. My sister,
eavesdropping on the other side, takes a hit on the nose
and staggers out from behind the door. I glare at her.

Music, literature, languages, I tell the social worker. My
mother opened those doors. I am grateful.

This is not untrue. My sister feels differently. She has
her truth and I have mine but she isn't the one doing the
talking right now. She is standing in the doorway practic-
ing the first hand position we rehearsed, the one indicating
a normal range of emotional responses.

Ah yes. Knowledge, says the social worker. Cul-
ture. The world. You must have so enjoyed your time in
Venezuela.

Clever girl, to go fishing like that. My mother has told
her the tale about Interpol looking for me in South America. She has been telling the neighbors the same tale and it
will take them some time to open their doors to me.

Before he got old, my father was a great dry-fly fish-
erman. It was his communion, those mountain moments

immobile in his khaki hip waders in the icy brook, the almost imperceptible flick of his fly rod sending the lure to land weightlessly, a dragonfly settling on the lip of the current, just within reach of the trout resting in the brown shallows under the overhanging rock, facing upstream.

I've watched a master do it. This little bureaucrat is going to have to do better than that.

I am suddenly lie-on-the-floor tired. My eyelids are lined with ground glass from opening into the wrong light in the wrong time zone, my lips are chapped and my hair is standing straight up, shocked to attention by the negative relative humidity of the western prairie microclimate.

Reassure me, I say to my sister. Did any one of us ever live in Venezuela?

No, she says. Lots of places, but not there.

Banks of fog, impenetrable to the untrained eye, lie across questions of where in the world we have been, fog that makes you stumble, hands straight out in front of you. And that's not all. The glare of black ice obscures other matters: who we are; what we are.

I am at home in the fog. I have several names, like all operatives with successful trajectories, and I negotiate the fog under cover of one or the other. I don't answer to any of them.

I grow up with three first names in Canada, where official documents allow only two. Three is uppity, punished by having to squish the third name in the margin and then getting your form refused as not standard. I take to pretending I do not have a third name, because it is twee, and because only my first two names matter.

My first name is my mother's first name.

My middle name, the one I am known by when we are out to impress, is Victoire. It's ceremonial. Victoire was Louis XV's fifth daughter and is probably the one who actually said the poor should try eating cake. She was quoted out of context.

Ah, here is Victoire, my mother says when I arrive home from school. She turns to the lady on the sofa and sets her teacup down, freeing her hands and smiling blindingly, back past her canines. Victoire is so fond of Henry James, she tells her guest.

I rein myself in. I do not check over my shoulder to see if there is a simpering doppelganger hovering there, holding a paperback to her chest, someone my mother could like.

I am not fond of Henry. I have not met him yet, and I won't like him when I do.

I am fourteen. The boys I like are called Duke, or Bruce, and I keep them well away from here. They brood and slouch against the lockers in the hallways of my high school. Sometimes they throw pebbles at my window late at night so that we can go make out under the lilac bushes beside the artificial lake in front of the Provincial Legislative Building.

Democracy in action; checks and balances. They work vigorously at getting to second base, and I foil their moves like a fencer—there are conventions—until finally they ejaculate, you can hardly call it premature except that this whole thing is pretty premature, on my skirt. We sigh and breathe in the scent of lilacs that drifts headily down to us like a blessing and reminds us we are mortal, and tiny mauve blossoms settle on our faces.

My sister has only two names, parental fatigue or failure of the imagination, and she too is known by her second name. Her first name is the name of my father's young sister, dead at five when he was at university.

Maybe she figures she was shortchanged with two names to my three. I figure she wins, but my aristocratic homonym would explain her tendency to call me Princess. Witness the following.

I am preparing to leave the luminous December skies of Sydney for Okotoks, informed of my mother's ill hap and my father's predicament, honoring a commitment made absentmindedly years ago to my sister that I never dreamed would be called in.

I feel she has strained for years, jumping again and again like a terrier, trying to see over the wall of their rejection. We've been disowned and disinherited. There's no changing it, I say. When something bad happens to them, we'll know soon enough and we'll deal with it together.

I don't realize it at the time, but when I say that, I imply I care. I imply there may be something to be salvaged. I misspeak.

But I'm flying there anyhow. So is my sister. Blood calls to blood. What can I tell you?

After I pick you up at the airport, my sister says on the phone, we'll stop at the mall and rent two carpet steamers and do the whole house. She has just told me that her partner, a competent woman who would make short work of a houseful of carpet I am sure, is not coming to Okotoks with her. She'll remain at home to run the property business they set up in retirement.

What an opportunity, my sister adds.

Not one I want to take up, I say. I'm not coming for household maintenance. You're probably not going to like it, but you'll have to step away from the Windex when I'm around. I have chemical sensitivities, reactions to parabens. I know it's boring.

You're such a princess, she says.

I am not flying halfway around the world to extrude cat pee from a Berber blend, I say. I will pay someone to do it, steam only, but it won't be me. And it will cost. It's like when you order a half-caf, low-fat, no-dairy cappuccino, hold the chocolate. It costs more the more you subtract, like you are paying for their brains to work backward and adapt. Same for carpets.

Okay, okay, she mutters. Princess.

I land and walk down the concourse of Calgary airport with locals wearing shearling jackets and Stetsons, arms away from the body, wrists loose, like it's high noon all day long.

We drive to the shiny hospital where four days ago they tried to wire my mother's crumbling bones together, doing their best but no warranty, no guarantee of workmanship; where three days ago my mother, emerging from the terrifying hinterland of anesthetic to find her husband holding her hand, says to him things so brutal and of such piercing cruelty that even the nursing staff finally notice the old man weeping into his hands and send him home.

It happens, they say. With older people. They come to, and a whole married life of disappointment and bitterness slips out, like an organ escaping an incision, like a balloon filled with acid. It bursts on impact, burning holes in their spouses' clothing and leaving little round scars on their flesh that never heal completely. Come back in three days.

So here we are.

We advance three abreast down the kilometer of gray linoleum: my sister, me, and my father in a wheelchair pushed by a gentleman who seems to be my formerly gregarious dad's only friend, a local officeholder and fellow campaigner for clean water, saddled by my parents with legal responsibility for all decisions concerning their welfare.

We come down the home stretch of corridor to my mother's room and a line of hospital personnel forms along the wall.

A nurse steps out from the line and asks which of us is the famous author. Heads come forward like turtles' so as not to miss a bon mot should somebody utter one. They wait for an answer.

I look at my sister. What? I say. She has her face in her

scarf, shaking like someone with ague. She gets a grip and hisses at me, You're the one with plausible deniability. Just say something.

Okay, I tell the nurse, here's the thing. I write but nobody knows me. I am totally unknown, even among my friends. Actually, I don't even write all that much anymore.

The nurse claps her hands in delight and turns to the others. Now, she exclaims, isn't that something!

To me she says, That's exactly how your mother told us you would react. You're so modest, you will deny everything. She lets out a little shriek. So do I. Nobody moves.

I could sign something if you like, I say, to break the silence. Oh, no, no, she says, emerging from her contemplation of me. We don't want to detain you. And your mother is waiting. Just such a privilege.

She sweeps the wide door to my mother's room open and ushers us in.

CHAPTER 4

Which one are you? my father asks plaintively in those first days, at moments when I am alone with him, my sister somewhere else, polishing, spraying product on surface, rubbing, shining. Wax on, wax off.

I don't clean. My disinclination for this activity I call by various names: sloth, depression, boredom. It's not that I dislike clean. I like it when it is done, but I don't want to do it. I don't want anybody else to do it for me either. I make exceptions. I clean the toilet, I wash my clothes, but organized housecleaning is as foreign to me as saying a rosary.

My parents' house is not clean. Even by my standards, it is not clean. My sister arranges for a team of helpers, three in all, to come in. They will care for my father when we go back to where we came from, my sister and I. In the meantime, they will clean.

The first one pitches in bravely when we show her the fridge. She is sturdy and raven-haired, married, with animals. She played hockey in her youth, before life sat her down and layered pound after pound onto her wide farm-girl frame until she is winded by the effort of standing up. That plus the cigarettes.

Dad played too, decades ago. In unlikely fashion, they will bond.

Hours later, that first day, she whacks the fridge door shut and says, You want blow-by-blow or gist?

Gist, my sister and I say in unison.

Okay. At the back, nothing identifiable. It would take carbon dating. Had to sacrifice the crockery. Some sausages back there, those mothers were not coming unstuck.

She peers at us for confirmation that she has done the right thing. We nod. It's like *Lord of the Fridge.*

Toward the middle, she continues, a delicatessen period, bad idea. Mayonnaise does not age well. Why grow your own penicillin when the pharmaceutical complex will do it for you? Anyhoo, she shakes her head, whatever.

At the front, a semblance of normal, she says. Milk, eggs, butter, dated within living memory.

She snaps her damp cleaning cloth. I saved what I could, she concludes.

My sister is silent, maybe thinking about how she would have gone about the job otherwise. I step in.

Thank you, I say with feeling. Please come back tomorrow. It will get better.

Count on that, she says, and lumbers out carrying the black garbage bags she has filled up.

꙳

Which one are you? my father asks me, affecting the crinkly twinkly blue-eyed pseudo-stern frown that served him well with the ladies in his youth.

I'm the one from Australia, I say, opting for geography.

You must tell me about the ashram sometime, he says.

That's not me, I say. That's the other one.

What's an ashram anyway, he says.

Not sure, Dad. You'll need to ask the other one. I say her name, the name she uses now. I do this because my sister changed what we were allowed to call her some years ago. She said that hearing her childhood name cast her back into the black chasms of before and we were not to do it.

Your other daughter, Dad, I say.

One day in a few months, when my sister and I are both back in our own homes, my father will sit in reflective mode with his helper and say, I have two daughters, you know.

I know, she says. I know them. She is flicking through channels with the remote, looking for the baseball. She knows there may be a meltdown if she can't find it. How about those Orioles.

He repeats it. I have two daughters. I adopted them after the war. That gets her attention. You what? she says.

Oh yes, he says. I adopted them. Sisters. And I hired a crazy woman to look after them. Had to get rid of her, eventually.

Crazy as a loon, he says, turning his attention to the screen. Don't have to worry about her anymore.

The helper will report this to us on the phone, fondly, just proof for her of her employer's encroaching dementia, which as it progresses, she hopes, will gradually make her the most important person in his life.

I will reject this angrily when I hear it. In my books, she'll be wrong.

I won't think, then or later, that he has dementia. His years will just be closing in on him, like the chutes the prairie cattle run through to get onto the trucks and then off the trucks and into the yard where they take their last free breath, the width of the chutes diminishing as they go, the last ones into the slaughterhouse just wide enough for one—no choice but to go forward to the end and to go fast. Move along, little dogie.

Life, the extremity. That is what will ail my father.

My sister will also react angrily to the careworker's sharing of Dad's remark, but for a different reason. She is angry that he said we were adopted.

I remind her that when she was little, she told people she was adopted. She wanted to be adopted. It was not an unreasonable position to take, I say, but everyone laughed, because you look so much like Mum.

He's disowning us, she says, her voice steely down the line.

Already done, remember, I say.

Emotionally, I mean, she says.

I'm not comfortable telling people they're wrong but I do it anyhow.

You're wrong, I say. He's claiming us. He doesn't want

anything more to do with the crazy woman. He needs us, but he can't have us around if we are her daughters too. We'd be tainted, dangerous and untrustworthy. But if he adopted us, he chose us. We're nothing to do with her. She can be, in his mind, just a seriously flawed child care choice. He can live with that.

My words won't help much. My sister will stay mad. She will nurse this new grievance like a seedling.

⇥⇤

But let's not get ahead of ourselves. We're not there yet. That's weeks from now. For the moment we are poised to enter my mother's hospital room, my sister and I, my father and his friend. My father may be casting about for confirmation of my identity and my sister's, but my mother has used the forty-eight hours since the nurses sent everyone home while she calmed down to fine-tune the roles we will all play in her little hospital drama.

She will be the devout mother, devoted to her wildly successful offspring who have flown incalculable distances to stand by her bed of pain.

Praise the Lord, she cries, as we enter. I falter, wondering if we have the right room after all.

She grasps my hand. You're here, she says. Praise be. You aren't too cold, she inquires, coming to this—she waves at the snowbanks outside her window—from where you were.

No, I say. I'm fine.

Kathmandu, I offer by way of explanation, meaning the shop where I bought thermal underclothing before I left home.

She can't know I mean that. She hears the word and infers some serious spiritual endurance training on my part. She turns a cold eye on me, assessing whether I have or do not have the chops to trump her surprising performance of piety with some more exotic ace of enlightenment.

Deciding in the negative, she nods deeply. All paths lead, she says, eyes shining.

Don't they just, I say, studying my boots.

Amen, says Dad's friend.

He has parked my father by the side of the bed. Dad sits there in his wheelchair like an old stork, his wispy hair electric from the toque he was wearing outside against the cold.

He holds my mother's hand, the one that isn't gesturing. Her nails are split and ridged with age and from the chemicals she uses to do something to furniture, something she calls antiquing. He still has beautiful hands, long fingers with perfect, smooth oval nails.

His eyes are bright as he looks at her, mute devotion to the moment that makes it all worth it—this moment when she holds the floor, radiating clarity and benevolence. People are silent around her, captivated. The moment when he can believe that whatever it costs, it is worth it to be enfolded in the aura.

I look around. I am the only one not gazing at my mother. It occurs to me that she is a kind of flesh and blood pyramid scheme, a human Ponzi. You buy in and you are hooked. You have an investment in believing the projections, the evangelical 3D laser image of personal power and aggrandizement, this illusion of depth in thin air.

I look at them and she looks at me. I know I am the only one who has liquidated the position, the only one to have taken the losses on the chin and sold up. It's hard to be sure, but I think she knows it too.

Meanwhile, back at the ranch, there are things to be seen to.

I leave my sister, who worked for decades in hospitals and is more than a match for the nurses and doctors with whom she confers, to discuss my mother's bones and character with them. My father and I catch a ride back out to the country with his friend who, in the hospital parking lot, insists I should sit in the front so that I can see the view.

It's okay, I say, I used to live here. I have seen it.

I don't want him cramming my father into the back seat of his little two-door Italian job. I wonder if cars have changed since I lived here. I don't think anybody used to drive low-budget Italian—not heavy enough on ice, prone to seizing in the cold. You needed big American or German. A Ford would start at minus forty. So would a VW Beetle. A Fiat wouldn't.

He insists. It's God's country, he says, as though that clinches it.

I look furtively around for cameras. Surely someone has set this God thing up and is filming for the Salvation Channel on cable. While I hesitate, he begins stuffing my father into the back seat. Dad is diving in headfirst, doubled over and groaning slightly, propelled by the friend pushing his bum.

There, he says once Dad is seated. He tries various combinations of belts and buckles to secure Dad in place.

What the heck, he says, giving sharp little tugs on a belt. Who designs these things! This won't reach. Now, how are we supposed to attach your father?

My father is rolling his eyes. I am for a moment unsure whether he is exasperated or losing consciousness. Either way, I think I would laugh if confusion didn't seem to be descending upon us with the darkness.

I point at the belt attached above Dad's shoulder. Try that, I suggest. Maybe they got that one right.

Could work, he says, and belts Dad in.

When we have left the big freeway and are zipping down the darkening prairie roads, he waves his mitt across the windshield and reiterates: God's country.

We roar like a sewing machine over the top of a hill and as we begin to careen down the die-straight two-laner, I see the Rockies. They shine, lit from behind where the sun has set, the snow covering them opalescent and a thin pearly band of sky above them holding the last of the light as the sapphire heavens deepen, the first star high above shining like a diamond on velvet.

If Jesus had been born on a ranch, this is what the three

wise cowboys would have seen. This is beauty you would follow where it took you, blindly, and it would take my breath away as it always has, if my knees were not jammed against my throat and we weren't beginning to slip sideways down the road.

My father groans. I sigh. This is no time for debate. The driver needs to concentrate on the road.

So I cave, and resort to the most common form of western conversational currency. Yup, I say. I clear my throat and say it louder. Yup.

Fishermen standing motionless in icy streams will say this to each other after an hour or so of silence. And if, in late summer, you could sneak up on the two farmers standing in the ripening wheat, rubbing the heads of grain thoughtfully between finger and thumb, if you could creep between the dusty stalks among the grasshoppers, you would hear nothing but the rustling of the grain and the occasional yup.

Somehow, somehow, we turn into my parents' drive, everything intact—the people, the car, the brittle little crescent moon above us in the black sky.

The snow is hardening, the cold settling in. My boots break through the icy crust as I leap out and swing open the big iron gate. If I were a child, I would step onto the lowest rung and ride in on it, but I'm not, and it's dinnertime.

My father wants the same meal every evening, and for the few nights he was alone after my mother went to hospital, he managed to make it for himself. He still wants to do that, so I hover and hand him things.

There is a chicken breast, pan-fried, asparagus boiled in another frying pan in an inch of water, carrot rounds boiled until soft in a pot and a potato nuked in the ancient microwave that hums and shakes ominously on the corner of the counter.

When I first arrived, I thought he might want some variety, some fish, a steak, but he doesn't. Starving people in camps obsess about the meal they will have when they get out, and I guess Dad is having that meal night after night now. He will brook no substitutions: no pine nuts, no snow peas, no crunch anywhere. Maybe a roast chicken from the Super Saver on the highway instead of the chicken breast, but that is his line in the sand.

I watch him shuffle across the kitchen, intent on his preparations, and my heart cracks. He was once tall and fit and strong, barbecuing T-bone steaks as thick as your arm on the patio, dicing potatoes to cook in tinfoil on the grill with a dash of Worcestershire sauce and salt and pepper, my sister and I sitting at the redwood picnic table, kicking each other in the shins, with a big wooden salad bowl between us: iceberg lettuce, avocado, crabmeat, ranch dressing. The Hallmark moments, such as we had, involved food.

I set the table and butter him a slice of Wonder bread, pour him a glass of milk. The dining-room table has a tablecloth, a lace overcloth, placemats on top of that and paper napkins on the placemats to put the plates on. When did they start doing this? There are two buffet sideboards in the dining room filled with silver and crystal, things we did not have when I lived with them, things that I have never seen. Where did all this stuff come from? What is it for?

I put Dad's pills in a little bowl in front of his place and we sit. He fingers them. What's this, he says, peering suspiciously at an orange one. My sister would know; I don't. I take a guess. It's your iron pill, Dad. It's okay. Those are the right pills. I got them out of the blister pack in the kitchen.

Out of the blue, my father says, I don't know if she can come back here.

I don't either, I say. We'll see.

I love her, he says, darting me a piercing little glance. He waits for me to say something. I certainly do not doubt that for a moment, I say, thinking that they would not be living out here and he would not be in this mess, that it wouldn't have been decades since he saw us, that he would not have trouble telling his daughters apart, if he had not loved her.

He lowers his eyes to the chicken. I just don't know if she can come back, he says. I understand, I say, and I do. He isn't talking about her hip and the quasi-impossibility of navigating in this house if you can't climb stairs. He's talking about the fear that she will come home and finish him off.

I know that's what he is talking about. I can't tell him that my sister and I are all over this, that we are using the breathing space our mother's hip rehab affords to have her mental capacities assessed and hopefully judged way below what it takes for a person to be released back into the real world. We will do our damnedest to make sure things come out the way he wants.

We'll do things for the best, Dad, I say. We don't have to worry about that for months. Just worry about your chicken getting cold for now.

We hear the dry squeak of tires on packed snow and then the slam of a car door. The loud slam of a car door.

My sister opens the front door and stamps the snow off her boots. A glacial gust rushes as far as the dining room, straight from the North Pole, bringing us the pure and unmistakable scent of winter, expanses of black ice and drifting powder snow carried by a whistling wind.

She steps into the dining room. Her cheeks are red. Oh good, she says, you didn't wait.

Yours is on the stove, I say. He was hungry.

I said good, she repeats. So, good. Good.

When I was little, at school, we used to cover sheets of drawing paper with wax crayon scribblings of color, until the entire sheet was a riot of waxy greens and blues and purples. Then we would brush black paint over the whole sheet and let it dry. With a metal teaspoon, we would do a drawing on the black surface, carefully scratching away the black paint to reveal the swirling color underneath, like the aurora borealis in the sky.

I have an idea that people are like those sheets of paper,

that every person is a black surface, jealously protected, but if you can get at the person with your spoon, if you can trace a bird, or a house, a tornado in the sky or a spaceship, and scrape the black away, what you will see underneath is the essence of that person, what really lives in her heart.

Scratch me and you get grief. It will well up surreptitiously and slip away down any declivity, perhaps undermining the foundations but keeping a low profile and trying not to inconvenience anybody.

Scratch my sister at your peril however, because you'll get rage, a geyser of it, like hitting oil after drilling dry, hot rock for months and it suddenly, shockingly, plumes up into the sky, black and viscous, coating everything as it falls to earth.

Take care when you scratch.

Looking around the kitchen the next morning, I feel touched that my father trusts us enough to swallow the pills we give him, the ones his doctor prescribes and which my sister has efficiently arranged for the Walmart pharmacist in Okotoks to package in a plastic folder for the whole month, all labeled. Monday morning, Monday noon, Monday evening, little compartments measuring out his days and our time here with him.

I am touched because the cupboards in the kitchen tell me that before my sister and I arrived, what he took was anyone's guess.

The Area Health coordinator arrives at the door and bangs authoritatively on it. When she steps inside, she sighs dramatically and tells my sister that they have been trying to get in here for years to help "these people." My mother wouldn't let them in. Hearing her clarion voice from where I am in the kitchen, I don't actually fault my mother on that one.

My sister brings her in to introduce her to me, explaining all the while that what we need is the roving nurse to take my father's blood pressure fortnightly and draw some blood every month for his tests.

The lady is not listening. She is taking in what I am doing, looking, as appalled as I am, at the incredible variety of alternative, complementary, and downright insane potions and powders and tinctures and capsules I am pulling off the shelves by the armful, sweeping them into the large black garbage bags that are my friends. I am keenly aware that these are my mother's dreams I am disposing of without ceremony. They are speaking to me and I can hear them, like people who pick up the local radio station broadcasts through the fillings in their teeth.

Good grief, the coordinator says. I nod. We really will need to know what your father was taking before you got here, she says. She looks at me disapprovingly, like I might be destroying evidence.

I consider this. No, I say, we won't. We can't know. Anyhow, almost all of this is years out of date. The only thing I recognize is saw palmetto. Maybe he took that.

She looks blank. It's for prostate problems, I say. Mum wouldn't have taken that, ergo, he might have. Or maybe nobody did, who knows. Or Mum might have, for that matter. We can't be sure.

My voice trails off. I am making a bad impression. Maybe she doesn't know "ergo."

Prostrate, she says, conjuring up for me an image of my

father reclining in a sunny field. How recently would he have taken that? What dose?

I wave my hands in the air like a stoner at a folk festival, to dispel the irritation I feel at this new manifestation of the human need to put a normal spin on whatever presents. I decide to show, not tell. I stride across the linoleum flinging cupboard doors open as I pass, to display the entire pharmacopeia, stacked up, crammed in, threatening to tumble out in a wave as I progress.

She puts her palms forward to stop me, like a traffic cop. I can see in her eyes that she is remembering who my mother is and that I am her daughter. I could be mad. Could run in the family.

We just need to know, she says coaxingly.

No, we don't, I say, trying for a tone of voice that will reposition me firmly beside her, inside the camp of the sane.

Look, I say, he isn't dead. Whatever he took, it didn't kill him. I lower my voice. She didn't kill him, I say, stepping on a tube of something and gliding smoothly toward her like a wraith.

He's not dead, I repeat.

I'm right here, Dad says cheerfully from his chair out of sight in the dining room, where he is eating his porridge. Bright-eyed and bushy-tailed, he adds.

And now my sister is escorting her into the great room to talk, casting black looks at me over her shoulder. Let's just try to move forward, I call after them, probably contaminated by New Age emanations from the vials on the floor. Have a nice day.

It's kind of a bottom-line situation here, I add.

Bottom, Dad says, reflectively. Where are my suppositories?

My sister maintains that medicine past its use-by date can almost always be taken safely. She is irritated with me for throwing out things that were best before 1990, a bit like us, and I'm afraid she might start searching for articles on the Internet, the kind with footnotes, to prove her point.

It starts much earlier this morning, as I am beginning on the kitchen cupboards. She sees me on my ladder with dust cloths wrapped around my arm, sweeping the contents of the shelves into bags, and tells me about the possibility of using out-of-date meds. She uses an expository voice, one you might keep for those who have not yet seen the light, to tell me that out-of-date meds probably don't work anymore, but that in most cases they won't do you any harm.

I laugh, thinking that she is still a funny woman. I am up on my ladder and I don't break my rhythm: sweep of the arm, clatter and clink in the bag, sweep of the arm, and so on. I am trying to finish this before Dad wakes up.

I only realize I have given offense when I turn around and she is not in the room. I go to find her.

Please explain to me, I say, why a person would take medication if it probably won't have any effect. Even if it will most likely do no harm. For my part, if my sole object is to avoid being adversely affected, I will just have a glass of water.

If I want my headache to go away, however, I persist when I should shut up, I want some results. And if I am risking all the side effects, I don't want the drug companies getting off on a technicality of date when I develop a persistent cough, clay-colored stools, and a propensity for cross-dressing.

We stare at each other in a surprisingly unfriendly fashion and I understand those family feuds in rocky, drought-worn landscapes where whole generations go by without speaking to each other. This is how they start.

So now, with my dad muttering over his porridge in the dining room and the sound of women interrupting each other in the great room, I pick up a bottle of 222s and remember popping these like Smarties in high school, when I had a lot of headaches. My mum took 292s, always ready to go the extra mile in search of superiority. I read the label, which is yellowed and doesn't even have a date, that's how old these little white pills are: aspirin, caffeine, codeine, 8 milligrams. No wonder I was not as unhappy as I might have been.

Ha, I say out loud, then clamp my hand over my mouth, thinking that laughing alone over spilled pharmaceuticals is only going to give the Area Health lady more ammunition than she needs.

What's funny? Dad asks from the dining room. I can't tell him the joke is that I don't need to feel embarrassed anymore about being the only living person who didn't take drugs in the sixties. Turns out I did, an opiate by any other name. And here I was a groundbreaker all this time, doing way back then what Hollywood celebrities and Vicodin would make fashionable forty years later.

I pour some coffee and go sit with Dad. He's forgotten the question, so we just look at the giant Douglas fir that he and Mum planted too close to the house decades ago. It has prospered, cutting off the view of the Rockies from this room, even though it never should have flourished. Conifers only grow this big on grasslands if they are planted over an underground water source. The water witch with his forked branch who surveyed the place when my parents moved here missed this hidden stream behind the house. The long boughs brush the windows when the wind blows from the west.

The tree is full of tiny birds, red-breasted nuthatches who live in it year-round and are members of a select minority of birds that can walk headfirst down a tree trunk. In summer they pull insects out from where they hide under the bark and in winter they live on the seeds of the tree.

The snow is shining like glass as it melts on the branches and the little superbirds dart in and out, faster than a speeding bullet. In the sky is the gauzy stratus-cloud arch of the Chinook that blew in at dawn, air warmed over the water in the Pacific Ocean and flowing over the Rockies from the west coast, bringing the temperature here up from freezing to balmy in six hours.

Dad goes off to root around in the bathroom drawers for his glycerine suppositories, and I put my head down on the table. I need to go into the bathrooms with black garbage bags once I have finished in the kitchen. I need to open the closets where Mum's clothes hang, everything in multiples, the same dress sewn by her dressmaker ten times in different materials, multiple fur coats, multiple shoe boxes full not of shoes but of canceled checks.

But most of all, I need to get into town today. I need to sit in the Okotoks café called Sacred Grounds, which is a pretty out-there name for Southern Alberta. I need a decent cup of java, not decaf. I want a blueberry scone too, a big sugary mound of a thing that weighs a pound and would leave the ladies of the Australian Country Women's Association speechless.

The trouble is my name is not on the rental car contract so I can't drive. My sister will, but only if we have a list of tasks to accomplish. I grab a paper and write: garbage bags, prunes, wine for her, more suppositories (what does he do with them?), a newspaper for me and a few minutes sitting in the steamy, sweet air of the café.

At the bottom of the list, giving in to despair, I write: front loader. To shift what is in this house.

It will come to that, down the track.

December wears on. It is dark at four in the afternoon. We can't stay here forever. We have lives.

But we could. There is so much to do.

I feel transparent, like a wonton wrapper in a steamer basket. The longer I stay, the less real I feel. I could turn out to be the daughter who never actually existed or, at best, the one who died years ago and whom they mourn, although my sister seems to have dibs on that scenario.

I sleep in one of my mother's bedrooms, the one where the mink coats are, under the jaundiced gaze of a flat-cheeked Renaissance Madonna with no eyelashes in a gilded frame. The walls are bile-green and the wrought iron carriage-lamp light fittings dispense a yellowish clarity that gives up and dies halfway across the carpet.

There are hats on shelves in the closet. More mink, right out of *Doctor Zhivago*. I can hear Lara's theme in my head each time I go to bed. And there are Bally stilettos lined up on the floor, long, straight-skirted dresses with set-in sleeves, pleated bodices, and pearl buttons at the neck floating on hangers above them.

There are two highboy dressers facing each other, one on each wall. Their shallow, elegant drawers are filled with carefully folded lengths of expensive dress fabric, yards of patterned silk and wool so fine you can see through it.

I almost understand this. The virtual garments contained in the neat folds of material are perfect, and remain perfect as long as the lengths lie folded, asleep and safe in their tissue paper, unpierced by needles, uncut.

I am reminded of a friend from my past, clearly descended from Vikings. Thick straight white-blond hair, heavy features but flawless milky skin. She refused to wear makeup, reasoning that someone looking at her made-up face would decide that this was as good as it got for her whereas, with no makeup, any degree of stunning was virtually there. It was all up to the imagination of the beholder. She ranked her suitors by how beautiful they imagined her, an accurate reading of how intensely they loved her.

My sister and I will go home, but in the interim I feel the need not to melt like Frosty the Snowman when the weather breaks and the thaw comes, a withered carrot nose and two raisins for eyes in a puddle of water the only proof I was ever here at all, plumpish and jovial if a bit underdressed.

I take to listening to Radio Canada, which broadcasts

Australian radio programs in the middle of the night, no doubt as a cost-cutting measure, the same way that in Australia we can hear the BBC in the wee small hours. I can't sleep and I want to hear Australian voices, like the fellow on the sports program I catch at 4 a.m. expounding on athletes making a shitload of cash.

I endeavor to explain to my sister at breakfast why I find this refreshing. She is shocked by the language and can't see why I prize this sort of straight talk, national broadcaster or no national broadcaster.

While I ponder how to make her see this, I admire two neat sets of animal tracks that bisect the fresh snow on the lawn, running roughly parallel and disappearing behind the bare-branched lilac bushes, one set bigger than the other.

Edge, I tell her. I like a little edge.

It's like the difference between AC/DC and Nickelback, I say, thinking that in these two rock acts I have found the perfect metaphor for the difference between my native country and the one I have chosen to live in.

AC/DC go for it, stamping and sweating, not caring if they are deaf tomorrow or if they dislocate their cervical vertebrae. They're not tall, they've got bagpipes and a school uniform, they're on the back of a pickup truck, they're melting the asphalt on Swanston Street and you've got to love them.

And representing Canada: Nickelback, tall and straight of tooth, nice boys, however borderline antisocial their lyrics. They always look like they might stop rocking to make sure their horses are properly tethered, that it isn't after 10 p.m. and they aren't too loud for anybody out there.

My sister turns from the toaster and looks at me. Who are you? she says. Other than that, she has no comeback and just hands me the toast.

Nickelback are from around here, I say. Just down the way. Hanna, Alberta, they hail from. They're brothers I think, some of them.

Dad cuts the crusts off his toast, as he always has. Edge, he says, smiling craftily at me.

At the hospital, we don't get edge. We get hostility from the nursing staff. It's not at all the same thing, not that anybody wants to hear my analysis of that.

The nurses are interested to know why we haven't brought our mother's things in. Do we think she can go on wearing a hospital gown and someone else's fuchsia boxer shorts?

I feel like I have just answered a knock at the front door and stand looking down at a delivery of dog poo on the porch, nobody in sight, sardonic laughter in the bushes. I have fallen into it again.

It has always been a strain trying to live with this. It's no wonder I'm tired.

One of the few coherent messages my mother repeated to me and to my sister as we grew up, a message she sometimes delivered with deceptive gentleness and a touch of sadness that we weren't more worthy prey, was this one, and I quote: I'll get you and you won't even know I'm doing it.

When you've been told, you shouldn't forget. The nurses' glares find me guilty of forgetting that my mother will get me if she can.

I try to explain that I have asked Mum, and asked again, what we should bring her, what clothes, what undies, what toiletries, a book? Does she want magazines, chocolate, a radio, socks?

She has told me that unfortunately she is not yet able to have her own things, that in this early and crucial phase of her rehab, she must remain in the hospital garb, including the fuchsia boxer shorts. It's protocol and makes it easier for the staff to carry out her treatment. She will have her own things later. I need to understand. It's different in here, in the hospital. She'll tell me when to bring things.

The problem is that my mother is supernaturally persuasive. She makes anything sound reasonable. On her urging, Mormons have been known to consume alcohol.

I did ask her, I repeat to the nurses, but I know how lame I sound, especially given the boxer shorts. My words echo off the tiles and the head nurse, thin-lipped, interrupts and tells me, baddie that I am in the eyes of anyone interested in advocacy for abused elders, that they need cardigans, cotton underpants, flat shoes for when she can walk, and slip-on trousers with elastic at the waist. Everything, except the shoes, is to be capable of withstanding sloshing around in hot water and bleach in the huge tumbrels that rumble night and day in the hospital laundry in the basement of this building.

Of course, I say placatingly to the nurses, of course you need these things. Of course. It's you I should have asked.

But I smother an urge to laugh dementedly. I could try to tell these women what is in the closet of the room I sleep in. Or better yet, I could tell them what is in the closet of Mum's second bedroom, where my sister sleeps. In there we have found what I look upon as voodoo vestments, I don't know how else to qualify them, garments hacked into with sewing scissors and pinking shears and left drooping on hangers like some senior-year high school art installation project gone horribly wrong. They scare the stuffing out of me, particularly one knitted jacket sliced jaggedly into ribbons from hem to neckline.

You can't wash mink, I mutter as I walk away, writing the list of items on the back of my checkbook. And just for the record, I add, somewhat unfairly, I might have thought to ask you if I'd ever seen any of you around.

I don't care if they hear me or not. It doesn't matter. Nothing I say could make these people like me less.

My sister knows where we need to go. We park in front of an emporium called Mark's Workwear and buy several jaunty outfits in velveteen, pants with elastic and jackets with Velcro, in what my sister calls gem tones, teal and maroon. My mother will hate them.

We go home to choose the least inappropriate shoes from those lined up in my closet, and to double-check that, in the shoe boxes stacked at the back of cupboards all over the house, there are no sensible shoes. We are pretty sure there aren't, as we have already opened most of these boxes and closed them again quickly once we realized we were looking at canceled checks, the evidence of my mother's frenzied bid to win her own money through frantic participation in any number of dodgy schemes, and to wound my father by spending all his money in the process.

When you write a check on a Canadian checking account, your bank honors it and pays the amount, stamps "canceled" on your check, and mails it back to you to keep or dispose of as you see fit. The length of a check is exactly the width of a standard shoe box.

On arrival in this house, my sister and I, surprised by the number of shoe boxes at the back of closets and cupboards, opened them to find not shoes but those canceled checks, thousands of them, paid out to gambling concerns, lotteries in foreign countries, mail scams from post office boxes in Philadelphia, Mexico City, several locations in Queensland and the Northern Territories, Pacific islands, places in Asia, dating back five or six years and representing an amount that would have ruined a lesser man than my father. We would have preferred to find that we were dealing with shoes, that our mother was, among other things, the Imelda Marcos of the western plains, than to contemplate this.

Now we go through the motions, peeking into every third or fourth box and finding only paper.

We'll buy a shredder, my sister says. What do you think?

I nod. Maybe a calculator too, I say. We don't look at each other, but she squeezes my hand and we stand together like that, looking out the window at the smooth blue surface of the snow in the fading late-afternoon light.

Christmas is upon us.

It's not like we haven't been warned. Every time we've gone out, all the loudspeakers at the gas station and in the parking lot at the Super Saver and all the shop fronts in town have been informing us, tinnily, that Santa Claus is coming to town.

His arrival is imminent, as is our departure.

My sister has sorted everything out with the helpers so Dad will be looked after when we leave, twenty-four hours a day. The only blank in the schedule is Christmas Day itself, when nobody on the team of helpers can be coerced into working 8 a.m. to 4 p.m.

This is perplexing to me, given that everybody knows a family Christmas will always go badly, that even the most extremely lowered family expectations will not be met. Magazines publish the same articles from early December on, year after year, on why we harbor these wildly unrealistic expectations of family unity, and how to avoid disaster on the day.

I thought that at least one of our helpers would prefer a microwaved late lunch in front of the television, watching *It's a Wonderful Life* with an accompaniment of periodic gasping from an old charge with sleep apnea having a nap down the hall, to a day of way too much turkey and stuffing, not to mention wine and beer, bowls of whipped cream hitting the kitchen wall in reply to real or imagined slights muttered into the refrigerator, and brothers-in-law taking it outside where they would do each other serious damage if they could just coordinate their swing and stop falling facedown into the piles of freshly shoveled snow scraped to the side of the sidewalk.

I personally would take the triple-time-and-a-half pay rate and the silent calm of the prairie night settling in over everything while it's still only afternoon, stars snapping tiny Morse code greetings from the icy reaches of the boundless sky, O Holy Night, but what do I know.

And this is the country, so Christmas Day will not be a problem. Here is why.

With my mother away in hospital, neighbors have taken to dropping in on us, as you do out here, normally. These are forgiving people and do not hold against my father anything my mother might have done. This is jaw-droppingly magnanimous of them, given that some of these people, in dealing with my mother, have found themselves up the proverbial. In one case, a dispute about a septic tank problem, perhaps literally.

They may also have other reasons, like a wish to see inside the house, or if my sister and I have two heads. Or an interest in the hay crop. Notwithstanding, props to them all.

Some of their reactions bear the stamp of interaction with my mother. Their shiny big all-wheel-drive vehicles cruise cautiously down the drive from the road and maneuver to park nose out, ready for a quick getaway. They hover on the doorstep even as we insist they come in out of the cold for just a minute, for a quick cup of coffee and a mincemeat tart. They keep their coats on, but bend to remove their shoes. It's like dealing with skittish horses.

New regime, my sister tells them heartily, new regime. Remain shod.

One who visits is ranching royalty, the mum of a big family from over the rise and down the road. My mother, in her will, has written about the parcel of land she and my father own out here, which she is not leaving to us and which, she writes, extends as far as the eye can see. This is delusion. Most of what we can see to the west belongs to the family of this nice neighbor lady, soft-spoken, the one who had to sort out the terrible septic tank dispute with my mother. Yet here she is, offering help if she can and commiserating about Mum, talking about the sadness of having to put a loved one into care.

You hum and haw, she says. You don't want to do it, to believe you have to do it. Then you do it, and it is better. It's okay. It's better than you thought.

She will fetch Dad on Christmas morning and he will have Christmas lunch with her family, with her and her husband, her boys and their wives and children, and she will bring him home in the afternoon for his nap. By the time he wakes up, his helper will have arrived for the first shift of the new order.

That's the plan.

My sister and I think about a little Christmas lunch for the twenty-fourth, just for the three of us, before she and I fly out from Calgary late that evening.

What to serve is a no-brainer. Dad is already tetchy about us leaving so, to avoid perturbing him further, it has to be the usual: chicken, asparagus, baked potato, with vanilla ice cream for dessert.

I know this is right out there, I say to my sister, but I suggest you and I go all festive on that chicken's ass and serve some cranberry sauce. You up for that?

She rolls her eyes. Just help me find the decorations, she says.

We poke warily into recesses in the house that we haven't yet begun to excavate, places on the too-hard list that we will have a go at in the summer when I come back. We are looking for evidence of Christmases past, a string of lights, an indication that they celebrated.

We find nothing but a couple of bent candles in a side-board drawer.

This is the part of the year when North Americans above the Mason-Dixon Line, and some of those below, are united doggedly in facing trips to and from work in the dark. Snow tires, flat car batteries, large square packets of snow sliding off roofs and thumping you, icicles falling dead straight from the eaves on your head, your eyelashes freezing together and snow over the tops of your boots. This is the time when your average Canadian Joe goes inside and feels a little better about all this by plugging in the Christmas lights and sitting on his sofa in the blinking multicolor ambiance with a few fingers of rye in a glass, straight up, no ice.

The Yule void in this house is sadder than the purely personal, sadder than being starved, or not seeing a dentist for years while your wife goes for checkups with no appointment, bursting in and demanding to be seen immediately because her husband is dying and she must get back to him. This lèse-tinsel is a denial of the deep cultural reasons for festivals involving lights and shiny things and piles of food and barrels of drink all being glommed together at the end of the calendar year: Canadian Thanksgiving, Halloween, American Thanksgiving, Christmas, New Year's Eve. It's because baby, it's cold outside, and dark too.

I try to make us feel better by inventing a little fiction, suggesting that all the Christmas things must be in the bomb shelter. We can't go in there without a decontamination team, I say.

We can't have a tree, my sister says. Who will take it down? Can you imagine? We come back in the spring and the tree has lost all its needles and is still standing there, lights blinking? Fire hazard.

We settle on a table decoration with a fuzzy-furred Styrofoam reindeer motif. No candles, because we don't want him lighting anything and falling asleep in the few moments he will be alone on Christmas Day. We wrap his gifts—books and fur-lined gloves. But what I would like to give him, and us, is something different.

What I really want is a fourteen-foot Douglas fir in the middle of the great room, baubles and candy canes and gingerbread Santas with hard icing-sugar frosting on their beards, tinsel you throw strand by strand so it drapes properly, a great big exorcism Christmas tree with candles blazing and an angel in golden robes on top singing, Rejoice! It's over!

There is now serious forward momentum. We are trying hard to tamp down the feelings. They well up like water around your boots when you step into a bog. We try not to feel how strongly we wish to flee, and how strongly we wish to stay. I say "we" but I am aware that I don't know what my sister is feeling.

I am missing mangoes and platters of prawns and lychees, photos in the paper of boozed-up Brits on Bondi Beach getting the sunburn of their life. I am missing my life far away, as far away as you can get. I know why my life is that far away, and what it has cost me to go that far.

We apply ourselves to the last details.

We take flowers to Mum. She grips my shoulders tightly in her bony fingers, and I can't help it, I think of Hansel and Gretel. She says in a stage whisper, I hope you have a good life. She says tearfully to my sister, I thought I had lost you. My sister and I are silent, in spite of the disapproving presence of the nursing sister. There is no comeback, or too much comeback—either way, there are no words. We are petrified in grief, like flies in amber.

It should end like that with my mother, with those two sentences, spoken into the silence at Christmas. It would make a good story, but that's not how life works.

We drive back to Dad's and make him promise again to keep his Supportline bracelet on. He doesn't want to. He says he doesn't need it.

The hospital coordinator has set this up, we remind him. She drove all the way out here to set this up. You have to wear it, and you push that big red button on the top of the bracelet if you are in trouble. They'll talk to you through the PA system they installed on the telephone and you can talk back, from anywhere in the house.

You promised, we say. You are a man of your word.

Oh, all right, he says. Yes.

In the airport, the woman sitting next to us in the waiting area spills coffee on herself. Oh fudge, she says, and my sister, giddily, pulls a detergent pen from her purse and, carrying on a nice little patter of information about how to use this instrument, banishes the stains from the lady's lapel to the bemused admiration of the other travelers, most of whom seem to be carrying animals in their appropriate travel boxes.

The employee at the gate tells me that they have relaxed the quota of animals able to travel on the flight since it is the last one out on Christmas Eve, and people do need to get where they are going with their pets.

Can you imagine, I hiss, the headlines if we go down over Kicking Horse Pass? "Christmas tragedy: plane lost with all on board, including four dogs, three cats, a ferret, a bunny, a toucan and a tortoise, and a partridge in a pear tree."

First my sister laughs. Do shut up, she says, and then bursts into tears. I walk her around the coffee island with my arm around her shoulder. It's okay, I say, it's okay. Just please don't faint.

sleep heavily and wake on Christmas Day stiff and cumbersome, like a bear from hibernation. The dawn spreads, chill and damp, over the flat suburb to the far south of Vancouver where my sister and her partner live and work. I see no wildlife from my window, just an occasional black squirrel breaking cover and barreling down the trunk of the weeping willow, before sprinting across the grass with its fur silvered by the micromoisture misting down from a pearly sky.

I am just passing through. I fly out of here tomorrow morning for Hong Kong to see my son.

There will be snow visible on the eastern slopes of the Rockies where Dad is, but here at sea level it rarely snows. We are just miles from the Tsawwassen ferry terminal, where you can embark for a trip through a postcard mauve and baby-blue seascape of islands and ocean to Victoria, the capital of British Columbia, or to Seattle.

If it does snow here, the flakes only survive in the air,

melting to mush as they touch the earth, which stretches like cling film across the water table, right there under the spongy soil, making itself felt occasionally by a quick bubble up through the toilet bowl, propelling a few drops onto the seat and the bathroom floor.

People move about here, walk and drive and shop, on this shard of the earth's crust that rests uneasily on the Queen Charlotte Fault, Canada's answer to the San Andreas Fault, which runs down the coast under L.A. and San Francisco. I don't like to bring it up, but I personally would not buy real estate here, as we are well overdue for a good grind of the tectonic plates and a millisecond away from liquefaction.

This suburb is laid out on flat farmland, street by street, the result of farmers selling one field at a time and developers progressively setting down a staggered grid of parallel lines and right angles, 44A Avenue and 55th Street, 44th Avenue and 55A Street, which never intersect predictably, an Escher maze with overtones of Kafka, all the more sinister for the neat bungalows and the occasional passersby, invariably pleasant but never able to suggest how you might get from where you are, lost, to where you want to go.

Beyond the houses are blueberry fields and expanses of potatoes with fragile white blossoms in the late spring. There are acres of corn and farther away, closer to the airport, huge greenhouses for strawberries, millions of electric bulbs burning twenty-four hours a day, lighting up the midnight sky with their brilliance reflected off the low clouds. Because there are always low clouds.

People from the prairies, where my father lives, often speculate that they might move out here to the coast to get away from the cold and the snow. Then they visit and soon go back over the mountains to Alberta, to Carstairs or Drumheller. You can't breathe out there on the coast, they tell their friends. The sky is down here, they say, indicating a level just under their chins.

I am just passing through and we don't speak of the last weeks.

We speak of the friends to whose home we are invited for Christmas dinner. We speak of the Christmas decorations on the houses that we pass, walking in the gloom of three o'clock in the afternoon. I am pleased to see the cascades of fairy lights and the reindeer outlined in green and red, the motion-sensor Santas who ho-ho at you as you come near. I for once am glad that Canadians don't understand conservation of energy and light up their properties in such joyous fashion. It's hydro energy, they tell me. Why turn it off? It's just there. This begs the bigger questions, but right now I don't care.

I walk like an invalid, like the survivor of a car wreck where everyone could have died. I shy away from breathing deeply, like I'm afraid I might drown.

The friends are newlywed second-timers. He opens the door, a big man, buzz-cut and taut, a dress shirt tucked in, pants with a pleat. He could be a former Marine if Canada had those. There's something a little wary in his eyes. He hunts, I will learn, and eats what he kills, a man who leaves tracks in the world.

His wife works at the sharp end of forensics. She is small, bright, and blond, used to seeing the end of trajectories. She welcomes me with a gift, a tiny pink rosebud preserved in acrylic gel in a cylinder, a perfect little "real" flower, the quotation marks on the box insist, that will last forever.

And since these welcoming people are second-timers, there are offspring: her daughter, a pretty teen who leaves at the end of the meal to see her "real" dad who, I deduce, is pretty busy just keeping it real. He's cool in the eyes of his daughter but, in my imagination, maybe chronically late with child-support payments. Our host's son arrives, a paramedic in a bomber jacket who kept his dad's heart pumping for an hour in the snow last year on a hunting trip, and got him back to the hospital for a quadruple bypass. Another man leaving serious marks on the world.

I love these people. I am full of an irrational gratitude toward them for having their own problems, their own parameters of fear and grief and loss, for inviting me in to see how this plays out for them and for giving me a chance to reflect on the nature of these things: that there is the visible and there is the invisible. There are the dangers and the difficulties you summon up the courage to deal with physically, every day, in the lab or the forest, and then there are the blows that fall from the air, unseen, unpredictable, but nonetheless brutal and crippling. Confronting the real makes you a person of substance; fending off the invisible that always blindsides you makes you Chicken Little, hoping to absorb a little warmth from the lights on the tree.

Another thing I did not know about my sister: she is not a fan of the mobile telephone. She does have one. It resembles a brick and is somewhere in her car. I think the only hope she has of using it for communication purposes is to throw it at someone.

So it is that we do not hear of what has been happening in Okotoks until we walk home down the blazing enchanted streets and listen to the message on the answering machine.

Here is how it went then, back on the prairies.

Dad has been to the neighbors' for Christmas lunch and is delivered home for his nap, as planned. Sometime into his snooze, he is woken by the sound of glass shattering, the panes of the French windows in the rumpus room at the back of the house, on the level below him; then the sound of the timber surrounds being torn out of the doorframe. Voices, not cautious, normal conversational level, and the crunch of boots on broken glass.

He is frail and has not yet regained whatever form he possessed before the imposition of my mother's calorie restrictions. He doesn't realize this, however, and his mind has been returning at a gallop, fueled by bananas and porridge, prunes and chicken and asparagus. In his heart, he's twenty and bulletproof.

He pushes the big red button on the top of his Supportline bracelet and from the speaker attachments now hooked up to every landline extension in the house, a loud voice calls from the hospital, miles away. Are you there? Are you safe, sir? Are you injured? Speak clearly. We can hear everything. Help is on its way.

As my father struggles to swing his legs off the bed and get into his slippers, he hears a lot of f-words from downstairs. Shit, man, somebody yells, you said no alarm. More f-words.

Dad grasps his cane and stands. As he progresses down the hallway, trying out the f-word himself, he hears the roar of a car with a dodgy muffler, the whine of bad tires spinning on the snow as the driver accelerates too fast. By the time he gets to the stairs and starts down, there is a knock at the door.

The Supportline contact at the hospital has phoned the list of neighbors we gave them, and here is the diminutive lady from two properties down, stamping snow off her mukluks and complaining about almost getting run down on the road by some hoons in a Pontiac. My sister will thank the universe for saving this lady from meeting burglars in a panic in a confined space. I am just glad her car was snowed in and she thought walking would be faster than digging it out.

When we speak to Dad, his voice is firm and he

expresses the regret that he couldn't get up fast enough to have at these weasels with his cane. We hear hammering in the background, the boys from the family who had him to lunch nailing sheets of plywood up over the broken windows downstairs. The police have been, the neighbors are there with leftovers, and the helper has arrived for her first shift.

We hang up and sit around the dining-room table in silence. My sister's partner looks grimly at the placemat in front of her, already set for tomorrow's breakfast. I want to reassure her, to tell her that she will not again be left to run the business on her own while my sister flies to the rescue, that I understand how hard that could be.

My sister takes a deep breath and looks at me expectantly. No, I say. I'm not going back there. Neither are you. I have to be in Hong Kong for New Year's, and you need to be here.

You reap what you sow. If Mum hadn't broadcast to all of Southern Alberta that they were richer than the House of Rothschild, a serious exaggeration, the criminal fringe wouldn't have decided that a Christmas break-in was a good idea.

Maybe, I say to her, you could look upon this episode as a sort of test run. All the work you did putting things in place has paid off: the system works, everything worked. The center has held. Dad's going to be fine.

One of the more reasonable folk sayings holds that as you begin the New Year, so will you spend the coming twelve months. It makes sense then to try to be clear-eyed and calm at midnight on December thirty-first, not unconscious or legless, or trying to walk backward down a hill in five-inch heels, or weeping inconsolably on a park bench. It should be a night of reflection, at best a night of marvels.

I am standing at the top of Mid-Levels, on a particular spot on Caine Road in Hong Kong, as I have on New Year's Eve at midnight for several years. From this place you can, on a clear evening, intuit the gentle curve of the earth, far to the north in the Middle Kingdom, way beyond the razzle and the dazzle of the jazziest harbor in the world laid out in the foreground for you. This view can settle your soul for the whole year.

When the fireworks start with a salvo of dragon eggs that crack the sky open and bang like gunshots before sparking all over creation, I stand with all the locals out doing as I am, leaning on the railing in the mild winter evening air that feels nothing like winter to someone from the prairies. Ah, we say in chorus at each chrysanthemum burst of lime-green and crimson, at each poignant end of a silver waterfall that starts so well, tumbling in a glittering sheet from the sky and then dying with heartbreaking grace. Ah, we exclaim at the whistle of the fuel strobing, at the profusion of dahlias and diadems, of peonies and bursts of blue popcorn in the corners.

All this splendor in the sky, this first marvel, would be enough—but wait, there's more.

The second marvel is that this place is not strange to me, that I am at home in the neighborhood to the west where my son lives, and where people occasionally greet me, Goodnight, mother, although we have never been introduced. No magic is involved. He is the only Westerner living locally and towering over them on the sidewalks. Who else could I be? Nonetheless.

Third marvel of the evening. My son, whose job it is to swim with aplomb in the dark currents of Hong Kong by night and to organize festivities for the privileged, has stolen half an hour from his busiest night of the year to wolf down a pizza in SoHo with his mother. He tells me some surprising things, economically, across the din of excitement in this little restaurant packed with revelers under the streamers and the disco balls.

He tells me that he feels we can close down the whole nature-nurture debate once and for all, through my agency.

With your family history, he says, peering at me to see if I am going to take this the wrong way, with your parents—if nurture calls the shots, logically you should be a serial killer. You're not, he adds reassuringly. You're a good person. You must have arrived that way, triple-plated.

Ergo, he says, folding a whole triangle of pizza into his mouth at once and looking at his watch. His mobile is chiming like the bells of St. Mary's.

Just for the record, he says, hugging me as he gets up to leave, I don't think you should go to Canada anymore. It makes you sad.

I watch him jog across Hollywood Road and up Cochrane Street toward his club, threading his way through party people two heads shorter than he is, shaking hands and kissing girls, the man of the hour who will wizard chaos into fun for them all, and my heart wishes fervently that he may avoid the shoals and prosper.

So here I am now, ten past midnight, on Caine Road. Aah, I say in unison with the others as an increasingly frenetic display tops off the fireworks, a this-is-as-good-as-it-gets, show-me-the-money kind of pyrotechnic last stand with just a barely discernible edge of hysteria. The sky is brocade, girls squeal and mobiles flash around me, fixing the moment.

The next day, as my flight to Sydney barrels down the runway for takeoff, shimmying and rattling, panting and humming and whining and trying really hard, the great big airship that could, I ponder the appropriateness of saying a plane lifts off, as though it were a weightless walk-on-water bug that floats effortlessly through the air and lands on gossamer legs without making a ripple. This is just plain hard work.

Some people live and die within miles of where they were born, and then there are members of my gene pool, wrenched from the surface of the earth and thrust up into the heavens in rockets to fall like bright filaments of spider fireworks in the sky, landing somewhere unlikely, who knows where, but none of us are in Kansas anymore.

And my son could be right about Canada although he is wrong in thinking, bless him, that going there makes me sad. I was sad already.

This most recent trip I will now try to recover from in the quiet of my Sydney suburb, where people think I am normal, has a positive bottom line nonetheless. My father is not dead. This result is delightful for me to contemplate and unexpected, given the way my previous trip had unfolded.

Come back in time with me to eighteen months before this New Year's Eve in Hong Kong, to my little green mailbox in Sydney beside which I stand, looking at a yellow envelope that has arrived with the bills. It has Canadian stamps and is addressed in a crabbed, geriatric hand that puzzles me. I turn the envelope over and read my parents' rural box number on the back, still puzzled because the hand that wrote this is not recognizable as my father's,

whose slim, slanted writing brings to mind someone trying to get close to the ground in order to be a less obvious
target, or my mother's, all confident pointed flourishes, a
martial-art-weapons script.

It is my mother, however. She who has not written to
me since well before our last face time fifteen years earlier
is sending me a thank-you note.

Your father wanted me to thank you for the Christmas
gift, she writes.

It's June, Mum, I say out loud. And you never thank me.

He can't write anymore, she goes on. If you want to see
him, the time would be now. Signed, your Mother.

I sit down on the grass. I think it's reading this too near
the mailbox that is making the sky wheel around me like
a Mick Jagger video clip, with bits of my life that would
threaten my standing as a normal homeowner in the neighborhood flashing in front of me. Including why I take the
mail from a little green metal mailbox on a steel pole and
not from the nice roomy one made of the same bricks as
my house that was here when I moved in.

Do you want this digression? It would be awfully long
and take us far away from here, so maybe later. For now,
suffice it to say the brick mailbox was mowed down in a
gratuitous act of postal violence by the father of my children as he backed at speed out of my driveway, calling out
to me cheerfully as he sped off that it was going to fall
down anyway. It had ants.

Never mind the mailbox.

Over the last decade and a half my sister and I have

tried to maintain contact with our parents, each in her own way. I send a parcel at Christmas, launching it into the December postal fray with about the same amount of hope and engagement that I would feel throwing a bottle with a message for Santa, or God, into the surf at Curl Curl Beach in Sydney. It's a ritual.

My sister has been more engaged, still believing that the people who begat us harbor a longing for family. She and her partner have gone so far as to offer to move close to our parents, to build a house near them and to help them when they come to need it. My mother has received this offer with fighting words, suggesting that any trespassing any-where near them would be answered with a Kalashnikov.

Faced with messages of this clarity, I tend not to go back for seconds. Somehow though, this shaky missive from the House of Loony worries me, calling up the thought of my father ill and alone. I phone and phone until my mother gives up and answers, and I ask to speak to Dad. He's out in the barn, she says. He's not here. His hearing aid isn't working. He can't come to the phone just now.

I try another day, and another, and she says the same things.

I don't believe her.

I'm going to have to go check, because my sister and I have long worried that a person snared in a situation like my father's might do a Peabody. Let me explain.

This expression derives from the untimely end of a stroppy peacock dumped on the Okotoks property some years before by an irate owner, and adopted by my father.

In summer, Peabody strutted his stuff, snapping his Arabian Nights tail feathers into a splendid fan, lecturing raucously and nipping at the cats. In winter, he was confined to the barn, and after a couple of winters locked up like that, according to my sister, he just couldn't take it anymore.

One day when my father went to feed him, Peabody rushed the door and flew up onto a bare branch where no one could reach him, free again. Nothing could entice him from his perch. He stayed out all night in temperatures well below freezing, deaf to my father's pleas, and by morning he was frozen on the bough. I imagine his talons rotating on the icy branch until he hangs head down in the pale ice-blue dawn, frosty and as stiff as laundry frozen on the clothesline, before plummeting into the snowbank beneath him without a sound.

Here we are then, in the backstory, a year and a half before my mother collapses on the kitchen floor, her hip in powder.

Since receiving my mother's little thank-you note announcing my father's impending demise, I have carried an image in my head, a Prairie Gothic portrait, posed like the painting: my father, in the barn with the dust motes of summer dancing in the golden air around him, afternoon sunlight slanting through the rafters. He is sitting on one of his selection of ride-on mowers, bought to deal with the acres of rolling lawn and replaced with a new one as soon as anything went wrong. There is a line of machines parked in there, like a John Deere showroom.

He sits straight of back and as dead as his hopes for a quiet life, his flesh sinking inward and desiccating like an apple from last year's harvest, a cadaver's grin on his face and his hands at ten to two on the steering wheel of the mower. My mother stands beside him, her hand on his shoulder and smiling slightly, going for the Mona Lisa effect.

Her eyes look straight at me. You wanted to see your father? Here you are. Is this what you wanted?

So here we are then, up to where I am planning a trip in the face of surprising and sudden opposition from everybody I know. The heat is off a bit since I have actually spoken once to my father as a result of my telephone harassment initiative, and I know now that he is not dead, only almost—vague and uncommunicative and audibly panicked by the idea that I might come to see him. I heard the click when my mother picked up the receiver in the other room and so did he. We can hear her breathing. He is only deaf when he chooses.

Come later, he whispers. Later.

When you are dead? I say silently. I don't think so.

Out loud I say, Okay, Dad. It's all right.

I call my sister. She says, Why? Why would you go to see them? They hate us. They don't want to see us. We can't go. It's dangerous. There's a rifle and who knows what all.

She is still smarting from the fallout of a phone call we made some months before to the Mounted Police, who have jurisdiction over the foothills, in the face of dead silence from the property on the hill where our parents are holed up.

We decided they were dead, or dying and just lying there suffering and, with no family or friends we felt could go check for us, we sent in the cavalry.

The phone call my sister got from a nice young officer,

who tried to cushion what he had to say the best way he could, was a zenith of bewilderment and hurt for her, and she is not going to forget it.

He said, I saw both your parents. Your mother came to the door and explained that they still drive, that they have food and medicine and doctors and dentists on speed-dial, neighbors at their beck and call. I insisted on seeing your father. I was allowed to step inside. Your father waved from his chair. The only thing he said was—and here the young Mountie apologized—I am sorry to have to relay this to you, but your father's only spoken words were: "Those girls are just after the money."

My sister thanked him politely and dialed directory assistance to get the number for my father's sole surviving sibling. She phoned him and his wife, people with whom we had had no contact for years. She asked if it was possible that my father's pronouncement was true, that she was venal and horrible and completely unaware of her own motives.

Our uncle said, I have never seen anything to indicate that could be true of you, or your sister. Your parents, however, that fits like a glove.

I tell my children I will be away for a couple of weeks. My son is only aware of his grandparents as an elusive yet forbidding shadow following his mother around, but my daughter thinks I am a fool. She has had two close encounters with my mother and cannot believe anyone would care what happens to her.

I can hardly explain to my children that I am doing this in application of my principle of preemptive karma. I can't explain because I would need to tell them that this principle is also what guides my parenting, and this would lead to discussion.

You sometimes see photos of surfers or rock stars with tattoos that say things like "No Regrets," and you imagine this is an exhortation to live fully, even or especially to excess, in contravention of all healthy-living guidelines.

I suspect it is not that simple, that words are slipperier than that. I suspect that on a corner of my soul is a tattoo saying "no regrets," all lowercase size 12 Old Bookman font, and it means not excess but restraint.

It means always try to do the decent thing, the rational thing, the selfless thing, the boring thing, because then you won't have to beat yourself up with guilt until your early stress-induced death. Or, if my sister is right, all through your next existences as lower life forms paying for your sins, as a slug or maybe a bat if you are lucky.

Do nothing you know you will live to regret.

The most supportive person I run into in Australia is a disembodied voice when I phone HR at my workplace. She tells me she totally gets what I am explaining to her, and arranges something called compassionate leave for me, adding that I should stay as long as it takes and she'll handle things for me on this end.

Bless you, I say. Yeah, she sighs. Been there, done that.

⋇

I call my mother. She has become used to me phoning and sometimes answers if she wants to complain about the parlous state of the roof, the plumbing, the flooring; about the impossibility of getting a tradesman to travel "way out there," when "way out there" is not exactly several days' coach travel through hostile Indian country from the nearest foothill towns, or even from Calgary. I am suspicious and will travel with phone numbers for every social service available in Southern Alberta, for Meals on Wheels and Volunteer Drivers, determined to unleash the hounds of home care on their stubborn old behinds if I find them living like Norman Bates.

My mother says, You can't come here. I reply, with unbecoming childishness, You can't stop me. She tries another tack.

You can't stay here, she says. You'll just make work for me.

I don't plan to, I tell her. I'll stay somewhere else, a hotel. I'll come out to see you. I'll knock on the door. You can make me a cup of coffee. Or not, if that's too big an ask. We can go into town for a coffee. Or not, as you wish. Bottom line, you can open the door or not, but I will knock.

Why? she cries. Why would you do this to us? Why would you come here?

I hang up and answer the questions in my mind. Because you are my parents, more's the pity, and because I can.

I call my aunt and uncle. I remember their kindness to my sister after the RCMP intervention fiasco, and I would like to see them. They veto my hotel idea. They will fetch me at the airport, I will stay with them and they will drive me out to see my parents whenever I want. They act like family. They are family. I manage to stammer my thanks.

I stop in Vancouver overnight with my sister and her partner. My sister is humming like a transformer with something I take for anger at my deciding to do what I am doing. I try to explain that this is what I need to do, that she has no need to participate in what I've decided; that over the years she has made more attempts than I have to reach out and connect; that she has been consistently beaten back when she has tried. This is my go at it, I explain, and it's a one-off.

I completely misread her distress. I think she is hurt because I am making a decision without consulting her; I think she will get over it. A couple of years later, her partner will tell me that my sister packed a bag to go with me to see our parents and stowed it in the back of the trunk of her car, that she made a reservation to fly with me, to protect me. All the way to the airport she wrestled with herself, breathing deeply and steeling herself to do this thing, to go with me, but when at the drop-off point her partner took my bag out of the trunk and looked inquiringly at her, my sister couldn't do it. She shook her head, no, burst into tears and hugged me like I was going to war and she might never see me again. That is what she believed.

I saw nothing of this, understood none of this. I

thought she was simply overwrought. She thought I was a dead woman walking.

My uncle would have similar reservations about what I was doing. They weren't actually wrong, as it turned out.

I should have been more cautious.

At the airport in Calgary, as I retrieve my bag from the carousel, I see my aunt and uncle from a distance, looking as they did decades ago except for nice silver hair on my aunt and abundant snow-white hair on my uncle. They are holding hands and peering endearingly into the faces of all the middle-aged women streaming by them, regardless of height and ethnicity, and consulting each other about whether maybe that one over there could be me.

I can't have changed that much, I call out to them just as they see me coming. We hurry toward each other and embrace like Michelin men in our big cold-weather coats.

Leaving the airport, I ride in the passenger seat of my uncle's big car. We glide miles and miles south on the Deerfoot Trail, prairie on our left to the east and the city of Calgary on our right, like lichen spreading on the nascent foothills and a bouquet of slim skyscrapers planted in the middle of it, near the river. We stop somewhere wood-paneled and leather-boothed for a bowl of soup because I insist on taking them out to lunch, the least I can do.

I try to keep their grandchildren straight as we talk about their family, so many of them, and a dozen or more great-grandchildren. All I have to hang this information on are the names of my three cousins, and a vague memory of how they looked as children. I wouldn't know them in the street.

We're like the king and the queen, my uncle says, every time we see any of them, whenever they visit. Like the king and the queen. They smile at the fullness of their life: love and problems, success and loss, pride and a hefty measure of grief. A well-worn life fully lived, perspectives widening with each new baby, blossoming like one of those paper flower buds that unfold into unexpected beauty when you plunge them into water.

In their apartment, I look out the tall windows in the breakfast nook. It is only midafternoon and it is only late September, but the sky is steely with gunmetal-gray clouds and the wind has stripped all but a few luminous yellow leaves from the aspens in the park across the street. The slender tree trunks stand dark and mournful, the branches swaying like the arms of the bereaved on hearing the news. There is a dusting of snow on the lower slopes of the Rockies in the distance.

I have to phone my parents and I feel nothing but dread.

My aunt and uncle go discreetly into their bedroom while I phone. My mother picks up, not surprised because I have given ample notice of my arrival. She asks where I am staying.

I was so hoping she wouldn't. For a second I consider lying, telling her I am in a hotel. I could lie, I've had practice, but you know what? I am suddenly too tired to be inventive, too gutted by considering how my parents have lived and how others have. I'm a battery with no juice, and frankly I just don't give a damn.

So I tell her. I'm not quite prepared for the force of the reaction. Her voice comes burning white-hot down the phone line. I peer out the window, looking toward the southwest for a mushroom cloud. You get out of there right now, young lady, she says. You come out here right now. You can't stay there, with those people.

Why not, I say. They're family. They offered. You didn't. You expressly forbade me to entertain any idea of staying with you.

She hangs up.

My uncle and aunt break cover and I fill them in. The phone rings again and my uncle's eyebrows ask if I want to take the call. I don't but I pick up anyhow.

They leave the room again. Down the line, my mother rants some more and hangs up again. I go sit on a big footstool and my aunt and uncle come back out and sit in armchairs and we all look at each other.

The next time the phone rings, I leap up and motion at them to stay, please. This is their living room. This is embarrassing.

But this time it is my father's voice I hear, tight and colorless. He says, You have to come out here tonight.

No, Dad, I don't. Mum and I have talked about this, about me not staying with you, about me not making work for her. I just want a little visit. We've talked about this.

Just stay here tonight, he says. This is causing so much trouble.

My aunt and uncle and I sit silently for a while and I can feel that there is a whole lot that they would like to say, a backlog that they are too kind to air, a bit more than sixty-eight years of unpleasantness since the day my parents wed and my uncle, as best man, felt in his pocket for the rings and realized that he had put them on the table in the vestry of the church and ran back to get them, a delay of maybe thirty seconds in the proceedings and everybody smiling, nobody caring at all. Except my mother, who hissed that he had ruined her wedding, that she would never forgive him and never speak to him again.

Your mother cuts a wide swathe of misery where she passes, my uncle says as he picks up his car keys.

My uncle has me by the hand and it is a good thing because my brain is busy wondering if I am disassociating or hallucinating, and what exactly the difference is. He has driven me here, south down the highway from McKenzie Towne, where he lives, the car slowing to turn right onto Rural Route 2 with the metal mailboxes on the corner, and slowing more with each mile until we are crawling into the drive that leads to this house.

Your car is tired, I say as we pull up, to lighten the mood. It's carried me around a lot today. He pats the dashboard. It's not that, he says. We're good for a few miles yet. The car just doesn't really want to bring you here, and neither do I.

Hello, stranger, my mother says to my uncle as she swings open one half of the big wooden cathedral door that gives directly onto her great room, onto the grand piano, the vaulted ceiling, the chandelier and the fainting couch, the wide, wide picture window looking west to the mountains.

To me she says nothing. She looks through me. I calculate that I haven't seen her for eighteen years. I imagine
a series of self-help books written by my mother for other
parents for whom any child is a problem child. Book One:
*How to Foster a Healthy Sense of Self in Your Children (Not!).*
Chapter One: Why would you? Look right through them.
That should fix them for a while.

You're letting the cold in, my mother says. I take my
little bag from my uncle. It weighs nothing, as my aunt
has insisted that I take only the bare essentials for staying
one night and that tomorrow they are, as she put it, bringing me back to stay my two remaining nights with them.
My uncle pats me. Tomorrow, he says, and turns back to
the car.

My father is sitting in a wing chair. He looks caved in,
huddled. He hasn't moved or spoken, but as I go toward
him, something flickers in his eyes. I'd like to think that it
is hope, or love, or happiness. Maybe it's just the last spit
of life from an ember as it dies in the fire, leaving ashes to
crumble. I reevaluate and decide that perhaps Mum had
cause to write to me, and that he is dying.

But then she must be dying too. They are both as thin
as garden rakes. Scarecrows look better. I blink in the dim
light, realizing that if I saw them in the street, I would call
an ambulance for my father without recognizing him, or
this gaunt and glowering witch dressed in layers of expensive dark Viyella and sporting a shockingly jet-black bob,
who dogs my steps as I approach my father. She used to be
a big woman.

My father rises painfully and I put my arms around him, feeling only bone.

Supper is on the stove. I put my things where I'm told and go to the kitchen to try to help. My mother disappears and when I venture into the depths of the house to find her, to tell her that the water has boiled away in the pot with the asparagus and that I have turned the flame off under it, she surges silently from a dark doorway and pushes me with both hands, one sharp shove of surprising force that sends me into the wall. I bang my shoulder blade against the thermostat and refuse to wince. Ruined, she thunders. Your fault. Ruined.

I stand for a few moments after she disappears down the hall, shying away from the understanding that burst upon me when she shoved, an utter, blinding certainty: this is how my father is going to die.

One day soon, he will open the door to the staircase leading to the lower level of the house. He will be going to see to the furnace or feed the cat, beginning to negotiate the steps with caution, and she will push. He will die. I see no way to stop this.

After dinner, as my mother cleans up, refusing offers of help, my father beckons to me furtively. I follow him into a sitting room, where he pulls a pile of photos from a drawer, pictures of my children, his grandchildren, that I have sent over the years.

You should take these back, he says. They'll be lost if you leave them here. Put them in your bag.

I do as he asks and when I come back to sit with him, he tells me a story about his war years. My father wanted to be a pilot, but he had astigmatism and rules were rules. He remained a flight engineer and never flew officially, even though he says he flew rings around the guys with twenty-twenty vision who went to fight the Battle of Britain and never came home.

Did I ever tell you about the time, he begins, as I remember he always used to, when I was flying with those crazy Australians who were training here? We were stationed east of here, on the base at Midnapore. I was up one day with this mad Australian, and he thought he was the cat's pajamas. He thought it would be a lark to land in a farmer's field, nice and flat, and go in and have a cup of tea with the farmer. No problem with the landing, although the farmer wasn't giving anybody tea after that stunt.

This Aussie still thought he was pretty smart, but he changed his tune when we realized there wasn't the distance to take off again, no way to get up to speed and lift off, even revving like the very devil was on our tail. Which he would be if we couldn't get this plane back in the air.

My father is looking far away, back in a moment when life was excitement and danger and possibilities, and he was coming to grips with whatever was needed. He tells me how he measured and calculated, how they removed some gear from the little plane to make it lighter, how he recalculated and measured again and came up with something.

If they tethered the plane to a rock formation jutting out of the ground at the very end of the field; if they tied it solidly to that rock and the farmer stood by with his ax while my father and the Australian in the plane pulled out all the stops, revving full throttle; if the farmer then severed the ropes in one go with his ax, there was an even chance that the pent-up thrust would propel this little training plane forward through the wheat stubble and upward. There was a 50 percent chance it wouldn't work and that they would crash through the fences at the end of the field, down the ravine on the other side, and explode.

The Australian said, We're dead anyhow if we don't get this thing back, aren't we, Jimbo, and off they went.

It worked. They catapulted themselves out of the harvested field and into the blue, whooping and swooping back down to wave at the farmer and give him a thumbs-up, extremely good physics calculations from my father and seriously flawed common sense and massive cojones on the part of the Australian contributing to their living to see another day.

My father sits, smiling faintly, looking at his hands. I wonder if he is thinking, as I am, that he has one miraculous escape in his past. I wonder if he is imagining, as I am, what the odds are of a second one; if there is the fuel to do it again.

There is a reason why people who live in the country go to bed when the chickens do, as the sun sets.

It's too lonely otherwise, out here in the thick black dark. No one can hear you scream. So immense and poignant, intraversable, is the distance between you and the one yard-light you can see burning on a property across the valley, so alien are you to the night creatures' real life-and-death dramas playing out with implacable predictability in the grasses and the trees around you, that you may as well just go to bed.

It's what we are doing. My father, too exhausted to speak, shuffles off down the hall to his room. I negotiate my way carefully across a stretch of parquet flooring leading to my room, feeling like Alice in Cuckooland and lifting my feet like a Lipizzan dancing horse, stepping carefully around pickle jars, cans of tomatoes, boxes of salt and bicarb of soda, and the occasional pot lid, all these disparate objects marking the spots where someone has tried to glue down the wood inlays that have come unstuck and lifted. These things are here so that no one will walk on these spots, but for a fleeting moment I wonder if it is an alarm system invented by my mother to keep me from escaping into the night, a fracas machine to trap me here. Even as I think this, I have a vision of my mother's influence making its way through my father's mind, filling the tiny spaces left by the rounded contours of his brain, solidifying around the synapses until not even his thoughts are his own.

I brush my teeth in a bathroom where a number of the white tiles with gilt flecks are held to the wall by Band-Aids of various sizes and types. The stretchy cloth ones are doing the best job.

From the doorway of the room I have been assigned, I can see into the big sitting room, where my mother is reading in the same wing chair my father occupied when telling me his war story. She has explained to me that she never sleeps, that she hasn't slept for eight years. She sits up all night, every night, in order to wake my father every half hour because, she tells me, he stops breathing. She told my sister this on the phone some years ago, and my sister replied that this not sleeping for years was incompatible with life. Missing the point, my mother agreed with her.

It's no wonder they both look so dreadful.

My mother is reading Isabel Allende in the original Spanish. She has always wished it to be known that she reads everything of importance in all the major European languages. She and my father journey regularly, I will learn, to a large chain bookstore in a South Calgary mall, where they have a personal shopper called Mary, who recommends books and orders my mother's foreign language works. This feat is seen by my mother as something akin to getting the Dead Sea Scrolls delivered.

Tonight, it is true that my mother does not move from this chair. I know this because the door of my bedroom doesn't shut and I have line of sight from the doorway. I get up and look periodically. Her head descends about two inches an hour until her face meets her book and her neck is at a right angle to the rest of her spine. She could snap something if she jerked awake.

This bedroom does not have happy memories for me. I slept here for one night eighteen years ago on my way to Australia, on a visit with my children who did not know their grandparents. I thought they should meet them and my mother insisted that we stay here.

I slept in this room in this same bizarre king single four-poster about a meter off the floor. My children were supposed to be sleeping with me but fell heavily off the edges. I settled them on the floor in quilts. My husband slept on the plastic cover of a white brocade sofa in the sitting room and my mother sat all night in the same chair she is in tonight, four feet behind my husband. My sister and her family drove up from the Badlands and slept in a camper van in the drive.

It didn't end well.

I don't expect to sleep, but I hunker down under the

same multiple quilts and crocheted throws as eighteen years before to ponder the weirdness at dinner.

To say that the dinner-table conversation was stilted would be to accord it a grace and spontaneity it lacked. My father was silent except when he rallied to respond to my occasional comments about the food, the excellence of the asparagus—a new bunch, freshly boiled, not the first, ruined batch.

Yes, good, he would say, raising his watery blue gaze from his plate to my face for a moment. There was a coyote in the fir trees a mile down the slope who was trying to help, but nobody was paying him any attention either.

My mother was clearly torn between two courses of action: freezing me out in total silence or demonstrating an off-the-scale graciousness and social savvy by rising above a difficult situation forced upon her by her daughter.

As I spoke of the carrots a second time, I watched these two impulses duke it out behind my mother's raven-black eyebrows. Social one-upmanship won out and she decided to make conversation, but this put her in as much of a pickle as I was for choice of topic. She was clearly not going to acknowledge me in any way. There would be no polite questions about the length of my trip or about how many children I might have now. And she was determined not to give me any information about herself or my father.

She began to speak at length about someone she called "our little girl," a toddler apparently, but so advanced, so good, so interested in the piano, sitting on my mother's knee and touching the keys reverently. At a loss, I looked to my father, but he continued to fix his cutlery, no help at all, as I tried to imagine who this child was.

My mother's monologue was interrupted by a rap at the door. This is the country and people don't just happen by at night, but at this point I would have welcomed home invaders. My mother disappeared and seconds later I heard a wail and cries of "Oh, no, not my little girl!" Alarmed, I rose, but found my father looking at me fixedly. He shook his head, just once, and pointed at my chair. I sat back down.

Long minutes of wailing later, my mother returned, looking composed and carrying a coffee cake, kindly prepared by people I presumed to be neighbors who must also be related to the little mystery girl. The child fell from a swing and broke her arm, my mother announced, and would be in plaster for the foreseeable. Shaking her head, she lamented this interruption to the child's apprenticeship of correct hand position at the piano.

When morning comes, I wake and realize that I have slept after all. I must have, because across the foot of the bed is one of my father's dressing gowns that wasn't there last night. It's paisley, put there by him for me to wear. I bury my face in it, hoping for a hint of his soap or his aftershave, but it smells of nothing. I put it on and go to breakfast. My mother is nowhere to be seen.

It is no later than ten o'clock when we finish and my

father tells me that we need to go out to lunch now, because we have exhausted my mother and she needs the house to herself.

Right now?

We have exhausted her, he replies. We need to go. We're going to lunch in Shawnessy.

As we leave, my mother appears. She tilts her head back, stares down her nose at me, and says, You won't be seeing me again.

You don't get to decide that, I say, and as I walk out the door, I hear her remind my father that we need to go to Shawnessy. Shawnessy is where we need to go for lunch.

My parents have an oversize town car which we don't take, and a big, posh flatbed pickup truck with a module on the back, which we climb up into. My father fumbles with the keys and tentatively tries shifting the gears. He has obviously not driven anything for a long time.

What's in Shawnessy? I ask. Why do we have to go there? Why can't we just go to Okotoks? It's five miles away. I'd like to see Okotoks again.

He doesn't answer and I drop it to let him concentrate on driving. I know he is concentrating because his shoulders are hunched up about his ears and we are inching along the middle of the dirt road that leads to the highway so slow we aren't even raising dust. It takes twenty minutes to drive the mile and a half to the stop sign where the dirt meets Highway 2.

My father indicates a left turn and suddenly I am incensed. Suddenly I understand why we have to go to

Shawnessy for lunch. To get to Shawnessy, you turn left at this stop sign, across three lanes of traffic coming toward you from Calgary, mostly eighteen-wheelers going to the U.S., drivers bloodshot and wired, speeding. Once you get to the median strip, you go left and seek to merge as best you can into the wall of traffic coming north toward you.

My mother knows my father cannot conceivably execute this maneuver.

I watch my father exert a feather-light pressure on the accelerator and we creep forward, perpendicular to the traffic screaming three abreast toward us.

I undo my seat belt and slide a bit to the left. Seconds go by like minutes as I try to calculate the tipping point, the instant when I will need to stomp on my father's foot as it rests on the accelerator and pray we don't stall, the microsecond when I will wrest the steering wheel from him and turn it a quarter turn to the left, just enough to bring us up on the grass strip in the middle of the highway without capsizing us.

I refuse without even thinking about it to finish like this, a smear inside the crushed cabin of this dolled-up pickup driven by a tentative old gentleman who won't survive this either and who hasn't been behind the wheel of anything for a decade. I won't be two minutes on the evening news and a paragraph in the *Okotoks Chronicle,* part of a prairie apocalypse of overturned semis with their wheels spinning silently in the pale autumn sunlight, a load of steel beams spearing across the road in front of people just trying to get to work, frozen beef carcasses waving their legs at odd angles in the brown grass and crates of chickens puffing bloodstained feathers into the breeze. I won't be condemned to a gruesome and spectacular photo-on-page-two death because of my senseless compulsion to try to do the right thing by my parents.

My father glances at me. Busy road, he says. Bunch of nuts driving too fast. He pulls himself closer to the steering wheel and floors it.

Holy crap, Dad, I say as the rocking subsides and he slows to what seems a normal speed to him, about twenty-five miles per hour, and we merge with the traffic going north which is forced to take a step to the right, just like doing the time warp again, in order to avoid us. I think we may have taken that turn on two wheels, but I am wary of embellishing like the heroes of old, who thought about how the song celebrating their feats was going to sound. Whatever.

Do your seat belt up, he says. That's dangerous.

No shit, Sherlock, I say, amazed at what is coming out of my mouth. I don't sound like me at all. I am momentarily unable to make a sentence that contains a verb and does not include poo. I stare out the window at a car that slows up beside us, the driver giving me the international sign for crazy out of your mind, forefinger circling the ear, eyebrows skyward. I reply with a minute shrug and an eye-roll, which could mean anything. Not even I know what I mean.

We're seeing a lot of nonverbal communication out here, since our Fangio turn. As irate people whoosh by us, some give us the finger. Those would be the folks from south of the U.S. border. Truckers too high up in their rigs for me to see them lean on their bullhorns with surprising Doppler effect, deafening everybody. Locals shake their heads disapprovingly and wag fingers at us as they go by.

You're in the passing lane, Dad, I tell him. You aren't making friends here.

I know, he says. I need to stay in this lane. I'm turning left again up there. He points to the horizon. When I whimper, he chuckles, and I figure just hearing that makes quite a lot of this worthwhile, but I will need to live to tell the tale for that to be true.

After some miles, there is a large intersection with traffic lights, left-turn arrows and slip lanes, all of which Dad negotiates without incident and we coast into the service road for the Shawnessy strip mall. My worst suspicions are confirmed. There may be nice places to eat in Shawnessy somewhere, and my mother may have been intending that we go eat at one of them, but on the evidence before my eyes, I don't buy it. We park in front of the Cheeky Chicken Diner—there is no dearth of places to park—and we go in. I object when the waitperson tries to seat us on spindly chairs at a table in the window. I ask for a booth and say that my father would be more comfortable there. All the booths are empty. There are only three guys having coffee at the counter.

We order the early-bird lunch special, it being only 11:30 and all. While we wait for our food, I go to the pay phone and call my uncle. He asks how I am and I say, Good, fine, well. Not dead. Could you come and get me? Maybe have coffee with me and Dad?

When I tell him where, he says, Why are you in Shawnessy?

Good question, I tell him. Or long story, or maybe both.

He clears his throat. Okay, he says. Sit tight.

I tell my father that his brother is coming to meet us. He isn't best pleased and just chews morosely on his chicken without responding, but I don't care.

I've always heard that these two brothers do not get on, never have. The story is that my uncle was my grandfather's favorite and my father my grandmother's, and this created enmity. I wonder why nobody ever mentions the oldest brother, a civil servant who, I was told as a child, hung out with trainers and jockeys at the tracks in his spare time and knew how to make money on the horses. Was he nobody's favorite?

I want to see my father and my uncle together, without my mother there to light the envy and stoke the resentment. I want to know if there is a spark of family feeling, an iota of affection. I need to see for myself how bad this bit is. I am now viewing my trip here as a kind of fact-finding mission, the establishing of a personal baseline reading on the scale of family horrible.

I'm arranging this little kaffeeklatsch for my uncle too, because I know that he has often driven to my parents' and knocked at the door. I know he has stood in the drive under falling leaves and snowflakes, and when the lilacs were in bloom, a man of all seasons positioning himself to be visible from the house, knowing they were in there and hoping his brother would show himself. He never did.

If I am honest, I don't mind that my father is annoyed at me for calling my uncle, because I am now seriously pissed off. A few minutes ago, sitting in this booth, I suggested to my father that when I see him tomorrow and the day after, because I am staying three days, he should drive to Okotoks and I can meet him there. No, he said. We've had a good visit. We'll leave it like this. He didn't look at me when he said this.

Up to now, I haven't been counting, not the money or the time, or the mind-numbing fifteen hours nonstop in a plane, over water the whole time, next to a woman who told me I needed to know that she had a problem with wind, and thereafter only spoke to me once, snapping the window shade up and inviting me to admire clouds that had to be, according to her, the white cliffs of Dover.

I have not counted my uncle's miles behind the wheel, my sister's anguish, the cost of facing down my mother. All because I got to see my father.

He won't get a hero's welcome when and if he makes it home, and I know he has to survive. There is no way he can see me again without aggravating my mother's anger. I understand that he has made his bed. I get it but I don't have to like it. I am the camel with the extra straw on it. So I smile and say, What fun for you, to see your brother. What a treat.

In Hong Kong, outside important buildings and especially banks, you see two big stone dragon lions guarding the entrance, facing outward into the world and scanning far horizons for danger, ready to pounce and protect, their manes etched flowingly into the stone they are carved from.

My father and my uncle look a bit like that, two old cats with still fullish manes of white hair, sitting in identical poses on either side of the booth, angled outward from it and looking at the hardware wholesaler on the opposite side of the parking lot, speaking sparingly of the weather and the traffic on Highway 2. I sit crammed in one corner of the booth and watch them, deciding that there isn't much to be salvaged and sorry I have put my uncle in this position. My father is inside himself, resentment rusted on.

They both look relieved when I finish my coffee and clatter my cup back onto its saucer. My father insists on paying, stands smartly up and heads for the cashier. My uncle offers to follow my dad's pickup truck back to my parents' place if I want to ride with my father, and to take me back to McKenzie Towne with him from the gate.

Thank you, I say, but there isn't enough oil in Alberta to get me back in that truck. Dad should make it home because he will be turning right the whole way. I'm coming with you.

⋇

My cousin, whom I have not seen for decades, cuts short a holiday in Montana, where she is driving around with her husband looking at Old West landscapes and artifacts that must pretty much resemble what we see around here, and motors back to Canada to see me. On the day left free by my father's refusal to see me again, she, her husband, my uncle and my aunt ask me what I would like to do.

I have done nothing to deserve the kindness these people show me. Although I am sure that the idea holds little appeal for them, they spend the next day driving me with good grace around the little towns of my childhood along the Cowboy Trail: Okotoks, Black Diamond, Turner Valley, places I was hoping to visit with my father.

Somewhere in the town of Black Diamond lives my earliest memory.

I am two, and my mother has set me down in the snow in the front yard of the tiny frame house we live in, to play. I am wearing a fire-engine-red snowsuit with a hood, white fur around my face, mittens caked with snow and a scarf across my mouth to breathe through so my lungs don't freeze.

I am sitting quietly, watching the diamonds the sun brings forth from the smooth surface of the snow, when a dark figure swoops in and scoops me up. I have no time to be afraid, even though I do not know that this big man, bundled up in his thick overcoat, with a hat and a scarf and gloves, is my father, back from some months working in the oilfields of Texas (just like Alberta, he will always tell us, only with more guns). He wheels around in the blinding snow and swings me high into the profound and hopeful perfection of the porcelain-blue sky. He is laughing and I laugh too, ice crystals sparkling on my eyelashes, little puffs of breath escaping through my scarf.

He holds me to him with one arm and picks up his suitcase. We head for the house. I try to put my arms around his neck, but the layers of clothing inside my snowsuit are snug around my limbs and I don't bend much at the joints. My suit is of slippery stuff but he holds tight and I know I won't fall.

Four years later, when I am six, the center of Black Diamond will burn down completely, a conflagration razing four city blocks of buildings, all the local businesses. I imagine my father hosing our little house down all night long to keep the embers at bay, as I sleep the sleep of the just inside, only two streets from the blaze. I don't stir as the flames light up the Southern Alberta sky just as the oilfield flares used to, burning off gas from the top of the rigs outside town, when the wells first came roaring in during the boom.

They will not rebuild the center of Black Diamond after the fire. Instead, they relocate disused buildings from nearby ghost towns—Naphtha, Commonwealth—towns that died when the petroleum industry moved to the new oilfields in the north of the province, at Leduc.

Waste not, want not. The abandoned ghost town barbershops and hardware stores, banks and appliance repair shops will be trundled cautiously along the foothills roads to serve again in Black Diamond, this flourishing little place, which remains today as hell-bent as ever on preserving anything of value that can be saved from the past.

Sometimes I am wrong. It happens to everyone. I'm not infallible.

I am wrong at the end of this lightning visit I pay my parents a year before my mother breaks her hip, a year before my sister and I fly to my father's rescue.

As I sit waiting for my flight to Vancouver in the Calgary airport where my uncle and aunt have brought me, I am pale with grief over a future that holds for me the certainty that my father will die at my mother's hand. This future I am imagining will not come to pass at all, and there are any number of verifiable facts I could be crying over instead.

But I am convinced that my parents are headed for doom.

I see this in terms of weeks, not months. My mother's rage will cause my father's death, or perhaps whatever is eating away at their formerly healthy and well-upholstered

Canadian frames, rendering them as thin and brittle as winter branches, will carry them off.

But I am wrong, and they survive the coming year, doing what they do. My father will turn off his hearing aid for good and get thinner. I don't know at this point that he is getting thinner and thinner because he is being starved.

My mother has always wanted to be thin, and during this year before she breaks her hip, she maintains her emaciated look with the aid of double doses, or perhaps triple, of the thyroid medication she takes for her self-diagnosed hypoactive condition, but I don't know this either yet. I know only that she says she has cancer in so many places that she can't even begin to list them, and this on top of something she calls terminal osteoporosis. I believe the osteoporosis.

During this year before she breaks her hip, she will continue to obsess over my father's sleep apnea, and to oscillate wildly between trying to starve him when he is conscious and waking him every half hour when he is asleep to keep him alive.

One winter's night, she drags him off in the wee hours to the emergency room of a hospital miles away, where they do not know her. The doctors find nothing untoward except her mental state, as she suddenly takes to beating my father up with her large handbag as he lies on a stretcher. She receives a letter some days later from the head of the ER explaining that she is not welcome in the hospital if she acts like this, because it is not their policy to allow a patient supposedly in some strife to be clobbered senseless by the person who brought him in.

My parents go on for a little over a year like this. My mother obsesses not only about my father's breathing but about winning what she refers to as "my own money," by means of the mail scams she spends her time sending checks to. Everyone should have a hobby. She wants to spend all her husband's money. That'll show him, she says. She also wants to win her own. She is having a red-hot go at it.

This takes some organization, as I will later learn.

She lost her right to drive during the routine road tests that over-eighties take to renew their license, the reasons being speeding in a school zone and avoiding sideswiping a truck only because the examiner grabbed the wheel. Since then she corrals neighbors and acquaintances from Okotoks to drive her in to Calgary to pick up new checkbooks and buy envelopes and stamps, or to mail the dozens of checks she posts every day at a post office she trusts in the city.

On one occasion, she commandeers a nice lady high up in the hierarchy of the local Heritage Preservation Society to drive her to the South Calgary mall so she can go to the bank for more checks. When they get there, this lady makes the mistake of suggesting that my mother might like to ride in the mall courtesy vehicle, since the bank is way off yonder down the marble concourse and she is worried about my mother slipping. Incensed at the implication of infirmity and age and decrepitude, my mother clubs the unsuspecting woman over the head several times with her walking stick. Before the shock and awe wear off her victim, allowing her to back away, she storms off.

The lady follows at a distance, holding her head and sliding behind mannequins and floral displays every time my mother turns around to see if she is being tailed. She certainly does not intend to drive my mother home and has a fleeting and, for her, uncharitable thought about how you put your cats and dogs in carry cases to drive them somewhere, and about how a model should be available for my mother. She has qualms, however, and can't bring herself to just leave her there.

When she sees my mother go into her bank and emerge a few minutes later with an employee who takes her arm and heads for the parking lot, this Good Samaritan decides she's done enough and walks off to do a little window-shopping, promising herself she will not answer the next time my mother calls because, really, she could do without the aggravation.

Late in the summer of this year, my parents' banker from that branch in the South Calgary mall, a conscientious woman who is alarmed at the gobsmacking magnitude of the money bleeding out of their accounts, and at the sheer insanity of the number of checks clearing, phones the property and makes an appointment to come and speak to them. She has done this in the past when there were investment decisions to be made or papers to sign, so my mother is not on her guard and does not prevent this visit.

When she realizes what the banker has actually driven out to speak to them about, and in spite of her rage at the impudence of this woman questioning her actions, my mother immediately adopts a defensive position of teary and hand-wringing contrition. She says she doesn't understand what she could have been thinking with all this gambling, and promises to stop forthwith. She protests that she hasn't been well; that she is old now and the grief of losing her one and only child, her little girl, so many years ago just gets worse with time, not better, an everlasting and deepening wound in her heart.

My father, I imagine, has the general demeanor of an old stag caught in the headlights on a country road. He apparently does not pick up on the issue of dead or living offspring, there being more serious matters to hand. When he worked, he had a finance department and accountants to calculate sums, to pay in and pay out, to keep things on an even keel. Since he retired, my mother has taken over this function for their personal assets. She has always been clever with money, and he has trusted her.

What shocks him now, as he stares at the embarrassed banker reading amounts from a printout, is not the number of zeros involved. His wife has always been an extravagant spender, and he has never begrudged her a penny of what she paid for the fur coats, the oil paintings by artists of the Group of Seven, the huge chandelier he abhors which hangs over the great room. There were things to show for these outlays, and a kind of grudging pride in him at the sight of his wife spending big, just because she could.

Now she is throwing money away, squandering it, a work in progress a bit like quilting, every day amounts big and small winging their way via airmail to post boxes in Malaysia, Queensland, Hong Kong and Florida, where the scam providers fish for marlin or play mahjong and laugh all the way to the bank. My father imagines the hard-earned assets he has nurtured and loves being eaten away, dissolving in an acid bath, and is appalled. Rancor blossoms in his heart.

Who knows what the banker is mulling over in her mind as she drives away, but I think we can safely believe that she is mulling. One thing above others sits badly with her in the days that follow and that is the dead child, gone for so long but still causing unfathomable pain, the blank emptiness where the offspring should be. The banker for some reason doesn't believe this for a minute, any more than she believes that my mother will stop writing checks. What is the Internet for anyhow, she reasons as she steps sideways out of her strictly banking role, finds my sister on the Web and contacts her.

My sister tells the banker that yes, she is the daughter of these people, and not only that—there is a bonus daughter, a second little girl, an older model but still in good running order, who has chosen as a life plan to live on continents other than America. My sister tells this nice, concerned banker lady that she must not mistake us for people who have any influence on what my mother may do, that we are disowned and disinherited, and have no legal right to do anything.

My mother intensifies her mail campaign rather than putting an end to it. My father works himself into a wraith-like lather because he knows this and cannot stop it. The one who doesn't care has all the power. Summer glides into fall. The leaves turn and the asters bloom. The Canada geese fly south over the foothills in impeccable *V* formation, high, high up in the perfect dome of blue, safe until they land. Along the Sheep River, the walking paths are paved with the gold of the aspen leaves, floating down on the warmth of the Indian-summer sun.

That will be the year that was, following my departure from this airport where I sit looking out the huge windows, drinking in the panorama of the Rockies to the west, trying to imprint on my retinas the line of the peaks against the sky.

I remember that every day at dawn when I was a teenager (except Sunday, of course—this is Alberta and nothing happened on Sunday in Alberta), the Calgary paper was delivered with a thump to the front step of the house where we lived in the city by a paperboy flying by on his bike. He never missed. I tried to get to the paper before my mother, who was always eager to compile her gallery of horrors for our breakfast edification: seals blown out of the water off Alaska by American weapons testing; unbelievable and tragic car accident stories ("Paramedic called to fatal accident on Banff Highway recognizes both children in the crumpled wreck"); cats up trees and babies with their heads stuck in railings. Four dead, my sister would mutter to warn me as we passed in the hall of a morning, one dog, one horse, two humans.

I wanted to get to the paper first to look at the editorial cartoon, but not for its content, about which I was totally unconcerned. I just wanted to start my day, before anything else happened to me, by seeing where in the drawing the cartoonist had hidden the little person looking toward the sketched-in backdrop of the Rockies, ignoring whatever else was going on in the cartoon and saying quietly, like a mantra, every day, Aren't the mountains beautiful today.

Sam Livingston had the right idea. He came. He stayed. The nine-foot-high bronze statue of his head, shining like a gold nugget in the prospector's sieve that is the Calgary airport arrivals hall, is telling you this. The plaque informs you that this is CALGARY'S FIRST CITIZEN.

He is wearing a battered broad-brimmed hat and his hair is long and wild, his beard tangled. Everything about him is scary and unkempt and dangerous except for the eyes, which give you access to a sane and civilized soul.

The sculptor who created this head obviously had something in mind. He hopes you will stand in front of it, that the face will fill your view and become a landscape. Those are his words. You look into these surprising eyes and you begin to wander around the landscape, feeling all the tensions of this place in precarious balance: wildness and decency; gritty determination and the whiplash humor that saw Sam delegated to represent Fort Calgary at agricultural fairs and expositions in Toronto, where his arrival in fringed buckskins, maybe smelling a bit gamey, would have scared the silk socks off the snug-suited financiers of the East.

Welcome to Calgary.

Except of course that I'm not arriving. I'm leaving after my three-day fiasco visit to my parents. I won't see Sam in the arrivals hall until next year, after my mother falls in the kitchen, her hip joint in powder.

Although I don't see Sam from the departure lounge, I picture him. I think about him staying here, calming down and doing something good after all his years of panning for gold and trading in buffalo hides with the Plains Indians. He settled. He married a girl and fathered fourteen children. He founded a school, maybe so that all those children could get an education, and set his mind to cultivating the rich prairie soil, bringing the first mechanized farm equipment to Calgary, the first threshers and binders that did not rely solely on the strength and sweat of humans and horses. He showed the Marquess of Lorne, who was Canada's governor-general, and his wife, who was Queen Victoria's daughter, around Southern Alberta's innovative agricultural landscape when they visited.

The people around the place didn't forget what he had done for them. His funeral procession in 1897 counted forty carriages. They misspelled his name on the tombstone in Union Cemetery though. The headstone has broken in two, vandalized, but when they repair it, I think they'll get his name right.

He stayed put, but I don't. My plane takes off and we

aim straight at the Rockies, the morning sun at our backs. Some minutes later, we lift just enough to clear them. I look down and feel the familiar jolt of surprise at how close the underside of the aircraft is to the jagged blades of rock that thrust up toward us, too steep for snow to cling to, slate-gray, angled and dark. The Rockies are less endearing seen from above, and you can't help but feel the full force of the unlikeliness of life. You know that all it takes is one capricious little updraft followed by a small but disobedient air pocket, which is nowhere near where it is supposed to be, to disembowel this airborne sardine tin and scatter us all, still strapped in our seats, along with the contacts on our cell phones, our suitcases and the photos of our children and the jars of preserves we are carrying as gifts, into the chasms below.

There would be no trace of us, no record of our individual travails or the titles of the books we were reading, the pages of which flutter a moment above the emptiness in a tiny tribute to us, as we disappear into this gigantic mineral presence and are no more.

Kind of like my memory.

Large periods of my early life are like that, like the blank bit that airplanes routinely plummet through and recover from. It's not that I have misplaced my recollections, and if I taste whatever Canada's equivalent of Proust's madeleine teacake is, maybe a chocolate-chip cookie or a Nanaimo bar, it will all flood back, all the bright, clear sights and sounds, colors and voices, and faces I loved.

It's not like that. My past is not merely faded, or camouflaged under the dust of years. It's not there, and I know a blessing in disguise when I see one.

I have managed to shake free and flee to far-flung places where I feel reasonably safe because I do not carry a lot of my past. My sister carries it for me, her foot in the bear trap of our childhood, unable to extricate herself no matter how hard she pulls.

I blanked it out and she didn't. Thanks to that blankness, I got the hell out of Dodge, while she feels the blows of the past continuously in her present. Let me give you an example.

Hair.

In all the photos of me as a child, I have long hair. I remember the painful dragging of combs through my curls, the yanking and tugging to get the braids even, the tight feeling at the temples like I'd been scalped.

I remember the scrape of the fine-tooth comb that came out once a year, to be used by my mother to comb kerosene through our hair after our outing to the Calgary Stampede and Rodeo.

There's no escaping family rituals. As a child all you know is that they are fueled by something dreadful and strong. You will try to come to terms with whatever this is later. In adulthood, my sister will attempt this coming to terms by adopting two Cree children. As for me, I will become a hypervigilant adult, forever on the lookout for the early warning signs of the ferocity that is in all of us.

We went to the Stampede dressed as cowgirls, with my father in cowboy gear. We weren't nuts. Everybody did this. The entire business community went to work in chaps and Stetsons for the ten days of the Stampede, and probably still does. We went to the evening show and watched chuck wagon races and bull-riding and calf-roping and ate fairy floss. I don't think we were ever allowed to visit what was then called the Indian Village to see the teepees, or to go anywhere near any member of the First Nations. Nonetheless, when we got home, the comb came out and we were deloused, just in case.

Hair.

As I approach my teens, I no longer have braids down my back. I would have been a hit as a Pre-Raphaelite or in the sixties with flowers threaded through my clouds of hair, but we aren't there. I have a ponytail I work hard at keeping smooth and shiny, and as I look at photos in *Seventeen* magazine, I imagine the freedom of less hair. I would like Audrey Hepburn hair, or even Lauren Bacall hair if I absolutely have to keep some length. Musing and speaking more to myself than to anyone else, I say that I am thinking about short hair.

I don't even see my mother coming. This was her strong suit—you never saw her coming. She has her sewing shears in her hand and as she grabs my ponytail, she hisses at me between clenched teeth, no one needing to hear the words but me. You want short hair, do you? Well then, let's give you what you want. Let's give you short hair.

I remember a moment's surprise that she would cut something other than fabric with her sewing scissors. It was a rule. We were forbidden from borrowing those scissors to cut paper or string or liquorice, anything other than material. They had to remain shiny and saber-sharp to do their job.

What did she do with the ponytail she sheared off close to my scalp? It must have lain intact in her hand, still held together by the elastic I had wound around it that morning. I wonder what she did next, because I do not remember. From that moment on and for a period after that, from the moment of cold metal against the back of my head and the crisp whisper of the blades closing, I remember nothing.

There will have been an aftermath. I will have been taken to a hairdresser, surely. What does my mother say to her? Do I go to school, short-haired—be careful what you wish for—tonsured like a monk?

No idea.

My sister, however, remembers. She tells me that she cannot, even now, pass a girl with a ponytail in the street without shuddering and thinking, I know exactly what it would look like if someone came out of nowhere with her sewing scissors and cut your hair off. She carries that. I don't.

I have had short hair for decades. My granddaughter tells me gently, her little hand on mine, that if I eat more vegetables, she is sure that my hair will grow. She doesn't believe me when I say I like it this way. She just shakes her blond locks and pats my hand.

I am in fact unfazed by bad hair days and even bad haircuts, untroubled by the sometimes startling results of someone mixing my color when not fully awake. I don't believe in skimping and frequent a reputed salon, but if things do go haywire in spite, or maybe because, of that, it's only hair. There are worse things, and chances are that I do not remember them either.

So, this flight from Calgary to Vancouver I remember clearly, the mountain peaks and then the Fraser River Valley leading us to the coast, the delta laid out flat, shining like silver and going, Yo, hey, look at me all temperate and fertile, you can even grow fruit here, no snow, why in blazes would you live on the prairies when you could be here, eh?

I do not remember after that—what I told my sister, how I spoke of my fears for my father, what I said and what she said, how I dealt with the reflex anger she must have felt toward me after the relief of seeing me exit the baggage area safe and sound. Nothing, until I am home again in Sydney days later.

I do know this: where there is nothing, there must have been pain. That's why there is nothing. Be glad if you forget.

Every story has a before and an after, a pivot point like the turntables rich people in Hong Kong and on the California coast install in their driveways so you can drive in and then, with a click of a remote, rotate the car 180 degrees to face outward, ready to loop back through roads already traveled but now seen differently, or to head off somewhere completely new.

This story does not feel like that, life being messy. There is a before and an after, but it is more of a watershed affair than a pivot point. One always hopes that the pivot point, or the watershed, will be a Eureka moment of blinding discovery, or even a gradual process of developing awareness, an increase on the side of hope.

This time, not so much. Here, the point where before becomes after is a banal and somewhat inevitable event, the result of aging: the crumbling of a large bone in the hip of a bitterly unhappy and vindictive old woman, getting crazier and more dangerous by the day, but who she has been and will become is neither here nor there.

This banal event will allow my sister and me the time to make sure she will be forever confined in an institution because she is mad, and to ensure she never returns to the property where my father is slowly recovering.

So when my mother leaves this ranch house in an ambulance on that cold December night, never to return, we shift into the after and begin to pick up speed.

The before was a very, very long run-up.

If we are doing life as landscape, think of it this way: the black and crevassed surface of the earth near the active Hawaiian volcanos, the lava cooling but still hot and dangerous, just a crust on the top, nothing you would really want to put your weight on. You could drop through into the molten surge below just by putting a foot wrong.

If you pause to look beyond your feet and raise your eyes, you see that in the distance, farthest from the volcano, the surface has hardened. It is black and shiny, making inaccessible most of your childhood, but you can distinguish from early on some signs of the long apprenticeship of duplicity that allows you to be standing where you are now, picking your way cautiously through life, not just a puff of smoke and a carbonized crisp of memory in the depths.

Here are two examples of how the lava of lunacy can pervade a life, even when you think you may have escaped it. One is from childhood and the other from adulthood.

Consider them bookends to any number of episodes in the struggle never to be caught off guard or to let crazy become the new normal.

Example one.

The autumn afternoon is warm even though the leaves are yellowing fast. People are listening to football on the radio. The crisp new apples are in the grocery store. My father is driving me to the drugstore to buy a comic book and he is in a snit. I have insisted on the comic book because I am to babysit my sister tonight and I want a reward for doing this.

My father is in a state of high moral dudgeon because I should, in his words, be happy to contribute to the family. It should be a reward in itself. Everybody in this boat rows, he says, grumpily counting three nickels out of the palm of his hand to pay for Dick Tracy.

I'm not fazed because I know full well that at seven I am much too young to be left in charge of my bumptious two-year-old sister, or to row for that matter. I know that he knows it too, and I figure he is getting off lightly, even if this is extortion. He knows that not everybody rows, that somebody is actually punching holes in the bottom of the boat. He is pretending not to notice.

Later, as they leave the house in a cloud of my mother's perfume to the *Bolero* accompaniment of her stiletto heels on the wood floors, she reminds me again that I must not open the door to anyone. If someone knocks, we must not open the door or even listen to what the person says, because it will be lies, all lies. If we knew what she knows about people in this neighborhood, she adds, if we knew half of it, we would understand why we must believe no one, never open the door, and be very afraid.

Well, hubris.

She comes home early, alone and without the house keys my father probably has in his pocket back at the party. She knocks and knocks. I stand behind the front door with her on the other side and converse with her, my heart pounding.

She tells me to go to the kitchen window and to look out at the porch. She will wave at me and I will see who she is.

I won't. I can't, I say. My mother told me not to open the door to anyone. She said that anyone who came to the door would tell me lies to make me open the door. In low and vibrating tones, she orders me to open the door. I don't, repeating that my mother told me I could never do that.

I am your mother, she says in those same tones that make the door vibrate. I don't believe you, I say. I don't believe you.

I learned recently that another babysitting incident about a year after this one is at the root of my sister's perception that she has always protected me.

The person who came to the door that evening was not my mother but an unidentified man. He had the porch light behind him and his shadow stretched diagonally across the opaque glass panel beside the door. He was wearing the kind of fedora my father wore.

I pulled my sister back into the hallway, away from the door. I didn't want him to realize we were there. I thought he would go away if he thought there was nobody home.

My sister, deducing from this retreat that I was afraid and unwilling to defend us, pulled free of my grasp and rushed to the door. In her biggest voice, she issued a command. Go away, man, she said. Go away. We're only eight and three.

We still see each other through the prism of this incident. Where I see in her a reckless propensity to rush in without thinking, she credits herself with a selfless determination to get things done. And while I like to think that I am rational and considered, she only sees procrastination and fear.

When I could, I took to fleeing ever farther, a moving target working at making herself fainter in the cross hairs, while my sister stood her ground, solid in appearance and stern, modeling her life like play dough. Neither strategy was successful.

Example two.

The phone rings in the flat I share with my husband and my two children, far from Okotoks, on a different continent.

I answer and find myself speaking to a friend from university, who is now working on her doctorate at the same eastern Canadian faculty where my mother has landed a casual lecturing gig, leaving my father to fend for himself for the better part of the last few semesters. She is trying this job on, as she has tried others over the years. None of them ever sticks.

My friend crosses paths with my mother on campus and speaks to her occasionally.

I am so sorry, she says. So sorry.

The friend and I communicate sporadically, in writing. This is before mobiles and Facebook and texting. For her to phone, it must be bad.

What's wrong? I say. Tell me what happened.

Your mother, she chokes.

I take this in. What did she do? I ask. I hear silence.

What do you mean, what did she do? my friend finally says.

What do you mean, what do I mean what did she do?

I mean, my friend says in a rush, she can't do anything, can she? Not anymore. She can't ever do anything again anymore.

She can't? I say.

My friend stammers, I'm so sorry. I know you must be so upset, this is so sudden, and I'm expressing myself so badly. I'm just so sorry she's dead. We all are.

You are?

I would have called sooner, she adds, but we've only just read the obituary in the campus newspaper.

I am at a loss. There are obituaries in the campus newspaper. I get a grip and ask, Why do you think my mother is dead?

My friend is sobbing now, trying to catch her breath. Not only, according to her sources, have I lost my mother, but I have also obviously lost my mind, maybe crazed by grief.

Listen, I say. She's not dead. Somebody would have told me. Even as I utter this, I realize I am not completely confident that this is true.

Your poor father, she says.

Yes, I say. Listen. Not dead. Not dead in any way.

She leaps on my words. I know, she says, I know. She'll always live on in your hearts. She'll never really die. That is the best way to see it. I'm sorry I've upset you.

I take the phone away from my ear and peer closely at it, in case it isn't really a telephone and I am not really having this conversation.

Not upset, I say.

Bye, she whispers. My condolences.

As it turns out, my mother had accepted two teaching posts for the same upcoming semester, one at this Canadian university and one in Alaska. She signed contracts for both and only then realized that, however superior she might be, she still couldn't teleport.

The obvious course of action presented itself to her. She composed a letter and signed my father's name. It informed the HR department of the Canadian university where she did not want to continue of her sudden death from unknown causes and her consequent unavailability to teach Intermediate French. HR sent my father a sympathy card, which my mother intercepted, and put an obit in the campus paper.

It's just a respite.

My sister and I know this when we fly out of Calgary on that Christmas Eve after spending those long days, those short weeks with Dad in the house where my mother's sudden absence is palpable.

We know it is just a respite. We have a little breathing room, but we mustn't lose focus. While she is in rehab for her hip, the other thing must happen. Her mental state must be evaluated and she must be prevented from returning home.

We have these few weeks of rehab to find a solution, to get a ruling that ensures she cannot be discharged back into the world to put her own life, and Dad's, in danger.

A broken hip doesn't come good overnight, especially when it did more crumbling than breaking to start with, and has been cobbled back together by orthopedic people with their fingers crossed. This is our window of opportunity, this rehab, our one shot at conflating the physical and the mental with the help of the authorities.

A broken hip takes time to heal and stabilize, if it ever does. Most old people with broken hips curl up and die within the year. My mother's doctor, speaking to me on the phone some weeks after my return to Sydney, suggested that my sister and I could probably stop agitating to prevent her return to the house where my father was because, statistically, chances were she'd never make it.

He didn't know my mother. I knew she'd beat the odds. He was also the guy who told me stories about how other families dealt with their burdensome aging parents. One family just bundled their recalcitrant father into a car, drove him quite far away to a nice facility in the country and left him there, the way some people deal with unwanted pets. Like Peabody the Peacock's original owner had done when he dumped him with my father. I asked this doctor if he was recommending that course of action and he said he thought it probably wasn't legal.

But before we get to that point, there is the rehab, more full measures of deep pain for my mother, the kind of pain you have to go through alone, like childbirth, except it is hard to see any joyful outcome at the end of my mother's travails.

And despair, because at some point there will be despair. She will realize that she may never get back home, that the wheels are turning to prevent her from doing that, and that my sister and I are making the wheels turn. She will have confirmation that she has always been right to hate us.

What will she do with the fury and the despair? Who will help her when she comes to see that her thrice-bedamned daughters, which is how she refers to me and my sister in a card she will soon mail to my father, might outfox her? How will she not explode into incandescent microscopic drops of blood-red rage running down the walls of the ward where she is trapped, when she realizes?

As I fly away, back to my life in Sydney, I am keenly aware that when I say that "we" have a small window of opportunity to prevent my mother from killing my father, that "we" must act smart and fast, I would very much like to mean "we," my sister and me. But I'm leaving, my sanity always dependent on living somewhere remote, so it is a kind of rhetorical "we." My sister and her partner will shoulder almost all of what needs doing, because I am so far away that my shoulders are purely metaphorical, and this is not fair, except for the following proviso.

My sister and I see all situations differently. When at this point I talk with her about what we hope to do, about arranging for our mother to live somewhere where she cannot hurt herself or others, about setting up twenty-four-hour care for Dad so he can stay on the property, because that's what he wants; when I talk about our efforts, I tell my sister that they are icing on the cake. Icing on the cake,

I say, when we get discouraged and nothing seems to fall into place.

I remind her that our parents have chosen someone other than us, an acquaintance whom we had never met, to decide everything about their health and well-being. Ultimately, years down the trail perhaps, he will be the one to decide when the hospital should pull the plugs and turn out the lights. When they were in full possession of their usual capacities, they legally decreed that my sister and I would be forever excluded from decisions about their welfare. We can, and perhaps should, walk away.

I have spoken to my sister about this because, however different we are and however badly she judges me, whatever gulf already separates us, she is my sister. I do not want the gulf to fill with the seething resentment she will feel because she is doing it all, but I know this will happen. I am telling her that I know this will happen. I know she will feel violent annoyance with me when I suggest something because I'm not there and I don't know, and I'm not the one doing it and I, on my faraway island continent, will sit quietly, gnawed by guilt.

We have nonetheless accomplished much when we leave that Christmas Eve, mostly as a result of my sister's lists and her beelike buzzing persistence.

The cupboards in the kitchen are clear of medication that is outdated, unidentifiable, deadly, or weird, and of tins of hardened cocoa from the eighties. There is a pad-lock on the gate of the property and everyone who needs access has a key. This way, if my mother manages to slip her tethers at the hospital, as she shows signs of wishing to do, and get a taxi out here, she won't be able to get to the house without calling.

The taxi companies have been warned by the security firm that does the perimeter patrols at night not to take her on board. The owner of the security firm is a neighbor, someone who has on occasion driven my mother into town for more stamps or envelopes or to mail her checks, and he understands. That he also used to be a very senior local civil servant doesn't hurt.

Dad has been introduced to new technology. The house is wired with a Supportline and he grudgingly wears the bracelet with the big red button on the top. He under-stands the dangers of identity theft now and has been using the shredder we have bought him with enthusiasm, turn-ing anything that comes to the house with my mother's name on it into little ribbons of white, muttering, Well, we don't have to worry about that anymore.

We have tried to explain that if an envelope comes addressed to my mother from the tax office or Social Security, from a doctor or a hospital, from a bank, that he should not shred that, but here we have not succeeded. He is soon muttering, Well, we don't have to worry about her anymore.

The roving prairie nurses from the hospital have been alerted, and will visit Dad every couple of weeks to take blood for the lab and check his blood pressure. Most crucially of all, Dad has the twenty-four-hour team of home helpers my sister has recruited. We feel confident that this will allow him some time of free enjoyment of his home. We can't really be faulted for not knowing how this will pan out.

With hindsight, it is clear that we should have known that people doing this home care job are often those who cannot or will not hold down a more mainstream job. They fall broadly into categories, each more alarming than the one before. Let me organize a little hypothetical parade for you.

Meet the housekeeping slut, obsequious and charming but, when left to her own devices, incapable of cleaning a pot or a pan (and you understand why, poor thing, as they are all caked and burned on, only to be restored to useful condition by the application of some power tools). Her exit strategy when there are no more clean pots and pans in the cupboard is to walk out the front door, leaving it open, and drive away.

Next is the mythomaniac, who complains bitterly about having to sleep downstairs in the cold with the mice, because we have supposedly told her that we will not allow fat people to sleep in the bedrooms upstairs. As nonsylphs ourselves, my sister and I stare at each other in amazement upon hearing this. We did not say that. There are no mice.

There is the gold digger, whose car needs urgent repair or she can't be sure of turning up for her shift. Dad wants to help her out and starts rooting around in his sock drawer and under the bed, where he has stashes of fifty-dollar bills. This person also begins to receive mail in her and Dad's name at Dad's address from a lawyer. We can only imagine that she is setting up some kind of de facto claim and hasn't realized that Dad is still married. Her long blond locks also cast a powerful spell over any man who crosses the threshold, and tradesmen begin wafting about at strange hours.

Then there is the serial killer, a powerful personality of a type my father is familiar with, articulate and capable, baking the best coffee cake south of Calgary. She manages to convince my sister that my father's diet should be revised. He takes blood thinners and has for years avoided leafy greens full of vitamin K, which counteract his life-saving medicine. Serial Killer tells us that the pharmaceutical companies have radically changed the composition of these medications and that now, on the contrary, it is imperative that Dad eat a lot of spinach and kale and bok choy.

In the time it takes for my sister to check, my father has ingested more greens than you see in the Canadian spring and his blood readings are zipping off the that-sharp-pain-in-your-head-is-a-bleed-bye-bye-now end of the scale.

As for the drug addict helper, he drinks all the liquor in the liquor cabinet, filling the bottles with water to keep the levels where they were, and steals the flatware one piece at a time. He has a similar pattern at home, but his spoons and forks are worn and bent—he must have gardened with them—so he will take one knife or fork of Dad's home each time he leaves the property, having carefully replaced it in the drawer in the kitchen with a beat-up one from his collection.

He will hallucinate one night, flying high all on his lonesome, and wake Dad because he thinks someone is breaking in. Dad calls the security patrol, who scream up the driveway and pound on the door. Once in, they assess and wrap the drug addict in a quilt and sit on him for a couple of hours until the sun comes up, he finally calms down and the druggie's colleague arrives for her shift. Dad goes back to bed.

But the one who will do us in is the one we trust the most, the stocky former hockey star who dealt with the fridge. She seems capable. She takes Dad out to lunch, and herself by the same token, but we don't care. She drives Dad around the foothills and takes him to meet the animals on the property where she lives with her husband.

When she takes Dad to see Mum in the hospital, she stands up for him, telling my mother that she cannot speak to him as she is wont to do. She steps back as my mother strikes out at her with her cane, reports my mother's verbal abuse to the nurses and wheels my father out to the car. The last time he visits my mother and exits the hospital in this way, a day that we refer to as Nuclear Thursday, he asks this compassionate girl if they can just sit for a moment in the car.

As he weeps, he tells her that he doesn't think he will come back to endure another visit. He says that his wife has told him to go to hell one time too many and by golly, this time he's going. She lets him cry, tears pooling in her own eyes, and sits with him, her mittened hand on the sleeve of his coat.

He likes her and we trust her. She phones to tell us everything. Two years later, she will be the last of the original team members, and we will have come to count on her. That it will take an intervention to wrest Dad from her is not something anyone could have predicted.

But we're not there yet. There is ice to melt and water to flow under the bridge before then. My sister and I are leaving, feeling cautiously confident that we have left him in good hands. We are tired and stressed and shell-shocked but we still, at this point, feel the hope of the exhausted worthy that our best efforts are not in vain and that we may be able to influence what will happen next.

Back in the sixties, people from western Canada would go to Mexico during the long winters, to get away from the snow and the ice. My parents started to do this after I left home, but my sister went with them. Mejico, my father would say gleefully on the phone, in an excruciating take on a Mexican accent. Rent a car, drive to the beach, play che-e-e-ken. I imagine him shaking imaginary maracas. My mother would spend her time buying silver and lamenting the sinking into the ground of the cathedral of Mexico City. She always had a nose for pathos.

Drug cartels, bodies in the sand and heads on spikes, not to mention kidnapping of holidaying gringos, took the gloss off Mexico and now large numbers of Albertans and Saskatchewanians and Manitobans fly to Hawaii instead.

My sister and her partner have for years spent February on Maui. They like a holiday with nothing to do but laze. They do not seek cultural input, but my sister's partner reads a lot, all the books she doesn't have time for during the year. They make it clear that they wish not to be bothered by anyone for anything that isn't life-or-death.

This February then, the February of the year I am telling you about, when my mother is still in rehab for her hip, is not different. The holiday is booked and they need to take it, this year probably more than any year before. I suggest that while they are away, I can help maintain the fragile new parental status quo in Alberta by stepping in as the go-to person for anyone there who needs to contact us: the hospital, the helpers, Dad's friend, the neighbors, the guy with the snowplow, the guy who takes the garbage to the dump, the guy who repairs the furnaces.

This is agreed. I may be in Sydney, but I have a landline, a mobile, and two email accounts. Piece of cake. We notify everybody that from February first, I am it.

Every day, I keep a log: phone calls in and out, who says what. I email enthusiastically and in volume. Some days I call my aunt and uncle just for comfort, and I call Dad every second day. I correct erroneous email addresses and leave messages for my mother's doctor at the hospital, as his message bank at his rooms is always full. I get the nurse at the hospital to write a note: could he please get in touch. I need signs of intelligent life. I need to know what is happening with my mother.

Occasionally I catch him. He rambles on about families strong-arming geriatrics into a home and tells me again about how old people with broken hips generally don't see out the year, so maybe we shouldn't be agitating ourselves so much over something that may not happen. I remind him we only have weeks, at best a month, before her hip rehab should be complete and she is good to go home, unless we prevent it.

Something seems cloudy and dodgy in how he talks to me, even though I sense sympathy. I wish I weren't a million miles away. I wish I could see his face and get a take on what's really going on.

I soon begin to fill in the picture. He tells me he has requested a psychological competency test. This could help us, but he warns me she might be deemed competent. If so, she could go home mid-March.

Underneath my notes for that day, February fifth, I write God help us, and I'm not a believer. I start to think about how to talk to Dad about this. I don't call my sister. Nobody is dead yet.

I call Dad every second day, but I don't always get through. He's asleep, or the helper is vacuuming and doesn't hear the phone. I know that Dad no longer has a phone by his bed, because Mum was calling at all hours to warn him to watch out for "those girls." That would be my sister and me, out to put him away in an "old man's home." Once I call during Ms. Gold Digger's shift and when she fetches him, he sits not on the chair but beside it, dropping onto the tiled floor on his tailbone. There is shouting and banging and the line goes dead. I learn that he survives and try not to worry.

I have rehearsed for a full day what I want to say to him about the possibility of Mum coming home, but when I speak to him, I can't see his face. I don't know if he is distressed or angry or sad. I don't even know if he has his hearing aid turned on and can hear me. I speak loudly. I insist he must think about what he wants to do. I reiterate that her coming home is only a possibility.

I imagine him sitting there, poleaxed because it had never occurred to him that he didn't have the deciding vote on whether she comes home or not, in the same way that we can never make him understand that half of what they own is hers. He just shakes his head. Of course I'll provide for her, he says. The best of everything, wherever they put her.

Our rock, the former goalie, has told us that he sometimes seems to shift after he speaks to Mum. He seems to start to believe again what she is saying about us.

Dad, I say, are you there? You call me anytime you want, anytime you have a question or you are worried. Anytime, you hear? The line goes dead.

He does call me a few days later. It is 4 a.m. in Sydney. He is audibly upset this time, and the helper tells me that he has just had a conversation with Mum. She told him that I had just phoned to tell her the following: I have decreed that she and Dad can no longer live in their house. They have to go into care; they can't live way out there in the boondocks on their own.

Dad, listen, I say. I never spoke to her. It's the middle of the night here. I was asleep. I wouldn't say those things. You can live there for as long as you are comfortable, but I don't think she can live there anymore. Isn't that what you and I have been talking about?

He mutters. He is a pencil's width from believing everything she is telling him.

Dad, I say. Think hard. Answer this. Have you ever heard me use the word "boondocks"? Can you imagine me saying "boondocks"?

He laughs and I relax a little in my chair.

After we hang up, I call the hospital and speak to the nurses on Mum's ward. I ask if they have any record of me phoning my mother. They don't. I tell them to get her chart. I tell them to write "manipulative" in capital letters, right next to the letters "MMA" my sister wrote. I yell that they told us she would be kept away from the phones. I tell them to do it, just do it, because she is going to kill him. I slam the phone down.

A few days later I have a memorable conversation with Mum's doctor. It isn't memorable because of any information he gives me, because we are still waiting on the psych consult and I still sense a kind of stalling reluctance on his part to fill in the blanks for me. That day, however, he is in discursive mode and has time to chat. The conversation is memorable for me because of what it says about my mother's ongoing magnetic manipulation of narrative.

Your mother is a bit down today, he says. I wonder about this. My mother doesn't do down.

What about?

She feels she deserves better, he says. You know, after

all her service to the country. During the war, he adds, when I don't say anything.

Which war?

You know, World War II, he says.

Any idea what she's talking about?

She's talking about how she hid all those people, he says.

My mother, in a note she posted to my father from the hospital at about this time, described this doctor as "a big man, not afraid of the cold." I picture him as a stocky, furry steer, digging his hooves into the snow and I am poking him with a stick.

What people?

The old people, he tells me. The old Jews. All the old Jews she hid.

I am glad he can't see me.

In Southern Alberta? I say. She hid old Jews in the foothills? What from? The cowboys? The bears?

With restraint, I suggest to the doctor that during World War II, the old Jews might well have queued up to get to Alberta and once there, would not have gone into hiding at all. I don't laugh but something akin to hilarity must be seeping down the lines of our communication, because he signs off in a huff.

I feel mostly sad after that phone call, sad that this man is now embarrassed by having been caught up in the magic web of a story she wove for him. I'm also in a way sad that she has slipped up. Any thinking individual is going to recognize the flaws in the saga of the old Jews in the Rockies once they step outside her aura.

She is seriously off her game, because had she told her doctor that she had hidden old Japanese-Canadian people, no one could prove otherwise. During the shame of 1942, under the War Measures Act, the government interned tens of thousands of Japanese-Canadian citizens guilty of nothing more than looking "alien." They took their possessions and deprived them of their citizenship. I'm sure there were people who were outraged. I'm sure some tried to help. There was an internment camp in Kananaskis, near where we lived. She could have been one of those who tried.

But she didn't create that fantasy, impossible to refute. She said "old Jews."

Two things happen suddenly.

First, the eminent geriatrician who sees Mum writes a three-page single-spaced letter. Reading it is like watching a skater on a pond: push to the right, push to the left, never tarry in the middle and don't commit to anything. He concludes that he doesn't have enough evidence to say that she is incompetent. The next sentence states that this does not mean that he is saying he is convinced that she is competent either. He ends that sentence with an exclamation mark.

His report details agitation, aggression, delusional

ideation, suspicious and difficult behaviors, decompensation and, possibly, a full-blown personality disorder. On the plus side, there is no dementia. She displays coherent and sophisticated thought, logic, and a sense of humor. In other words, she's a charmer.

More tests, he says. More evaluation. Give her "enough rope to hang herself" before deciding. Get input from family who visit on how she is. Give her day passes and weekend passes to go home and see how she goes. He concludes by saying he quite enjoyed interviewing her, and passes the buck to a competency assessment team.

Second, within hours of the specialist writing his letter, we are informed by the hospital that Mum has been accorded a place in a dementia unit in the town of Vulcan. They will keep this place for only a few days. The family must inform her. She will be transported from the hospital where she is to the unit next Tuesday.

I sit and try to put these two puzzle pieces together. They won't fit, although I now understand my mother's doctor's unwillingness to say anything definite. He works in the hospital where she is. He knows how frustrated they are with our refusal to talk about bringing her home. He knows how much they can't wait to see the back of her, even if she has to be sent to Hell—a dementia unit in a town named for the god of fire and metalwork and forges, red billowing smoke in the sky, when she doesn't have dementia.

Now I phone my sister.

Things happen before my sister returns to Canada from Maui in March.

The geriatric specialist who found Mum so charming and witty, in spite of her being (eventually, possibly, perhaps, probably) incompetent, opposes the hospital's wish to shunt her off to the first available dementia bed on the grounds that he has just written to them to say that, whatever else she may (could, might) have, she does not have dementia.

I suspect that Mum's doctor at the hospital has alerted the expert in a bid to help us, in spite of being miffed about the discussion he and I had about Mum's hiding old Jews during the war. He follows up with a recommendation of his own that buys us some time: that she remain where she is for more months of hip rehab, as she is choosing not to go to physio or therapy sessions and has been incontinent since her hip surgery.

He adds that she is unable to pull her pants up or down,

apparently some kind of defining criterion of one's suitability to be unleashed onto the unsuspecting world outside.

The geriatric specialist may have believed that he was very clear in his official report, where he refused to say that Mum was competent and refused to say that she wasn't. He obviously wasn't, at least not early enough in his document, because here is what happens.

The hospital team only reads page one of his report, ignores his recommendation for more tests and evaluations, and seizes upon one idea only: this expert could not say that my mother is incompetent. Ergo, the team decides, not reading pages two and three but dancing a jig and singing hallelujah, she is competent and they can discharge her. They schedule something called a patient conference quick smart, for late March, and request that my sister attend so that they can bludgeon her with this conclusion.

My sister is blindsided by this. She has taken her courage in both hands and fronted up here in Alberta to explain to Mum, in front of this gathering of doctors, admin staff and hospital directors, therapists of all stripes, why the family thinks that it is unsafe for her to go home, now or in the future.

The record shows that during this conference, Mum's doctor concurs that she should not go home but that my mother rejects this "vehemently" and takes over the proceedings, talking lawsuits, civil actions, and stressing the fact that she has enough money to buy and sell the doctor, indeed all of them in the room, at any time, and she will.

The hospital personnel try their best bully tactics on my

sister and keep pointing at the expert's report and chanting, "But she is competent," to which my sister chants back, "He doesn't say that. Read page three, read page three." It's like a Greek chorus. My sister's partner leaves the room at some point, and strides down the wide hallway to inspect the elevator my mother takes to the lobby every morning to buy her newspapers and flowers. My sister's partner is a handy person and wishes to inspect the elevator doors to see if there is any way to rig them to open onto a void when my mother pushes the button. She tells me this herself.

Back in the conference room, the hospital staff has executed a strategic retreat and, now pointing to page two, hammers at the idea that Mum should go home for day visits, weekends, (this is what the expert refers to as "giving her enough rope to hang herself"). My sister counters with the following tale. Since his last visit to Mum, on Nuclear Thursday some months before, my father has remained true to his pronouncement that he will not see her again. He refuses offers to drive him to see her with a polite, Not today. He never speaks of her.

Neither does he speak of his shock and despair, but we have the helper's testimonial about that day, and documentation from Black Diamond Hospital, where he is admitted with congestive heart failure shortly after that last visit and where he stays for two weeks, his body betraying how badly he is hurt, his heart broken and his sodium reading 20, which is the last stop before death.

My sister shakes for weeks after the conference, but she

has fulfilled her mission. My mother is not free to leave this place and go where she will.

The hospital understands that we will not take her away but neither will we allow her to be sent to inappropriate places. They expedite the second report by the competency assessment team, the one the specialist wants done before he pronounces conclusively.

To what I imagine is their considerable consternation, the report, once done, concludes that she is mentally incompetent, cannot go home, and needs to be looked after in a suitable place. This place will turn out to be one floor up in the very hospital where she is for her rehab, a locked ward with a pleasant color palette, airy common rooms, one with a grand piano, comfortable armchairs upholstered in florals and wide views over the fields to the mountains.

My mother does not give up. It will take many months for her to stop campaigning for her release, during which time she refuses all contact with family and tries to institute divorce proceedings. She writes heartrending letters to people she knew or thought she knew decades earlier—dentists and city officials, perhaps long since dead—whom she begs for help.

Her doctor, the big man unafraid of the cold, leaves the hospital soon after she is ruled incompetent. My mother wins over her new doctor, a young person from the Middle East, with tales of her money and her fabulous life. This person believes my mother and calls us when we are visiting Dad over the next summers to demand that Mum be allowed to come home. Why can't she, given that there are eight live-in servants? Mum's stories of privilege make sense to her, and of all the hospital staff who hate me and my sister and do not believe a word of what we say, she hates us most.

When the conclusion of the assessment team's report which seals my mother's fate is communicated to my sister, the first thing she does is phone me. I lift the receiver of the phone to the sound of jubilant crowing. And singing. My sister is singing something about the wicked witch being dead. She tells me she is organizing a party. I believe she is deeply disappointed that I do not join in; she is shocked by my shocked silence.

I feel only grief. I think of everything my mother will never see again: the view over the foothills to the Rockies from the windows of her house, the animals in the dusk light, fawns gamboling unsteadily, coyotes pausing to give you the slightest of nods before loping across the lawns that go on forever, all the way down the rise to the spruce trees she and my father planted in the seventies and that have grown straight and tall, shiny and strong.

She will not see again the things she found beautiful and bought and bought, and hoarded and hoarded, the silver and the crystal and the full sets of porcelain, the antiques shining with the patina of age, these things that were a rampart against her anguish, her fear, her anger and her desperation. How will she live on, I wonder. How can she?

Over the next summers, when my sister and her partner and I stay with my dad, getting repairs done on the house, keeping him company, and giving his helpers a few weeks off, I will salvage a few things before the dispersal of my parents' belongings.

My sister doesn't want my mother's first set of china, or what remains of it, Royal Albert Old English Rose, the old pattern, with much more gold than they put around the edges of it now. I remember it from my childhood, how it only came out on very special occasions, how those were my family's versions of good times, and I claim it. My sister packs it up with newsprint and takes it to the post office to send to my address in Sydney, where it arrives mostly broken. I imagine customs officers dropping the box because it has a label that says FRAGILE, satisfied at the sound of something delicate breaking.

My sister cries on the phone when I tell her about the breakage and now, years later, I am still angry, mostly at myself, for not insisting on a safer passage for something I wanted to preserve.

I do arrange a safer passage for a friend of my childhood, a large wooden rocking horse painted shiny black, with a leather saddle and stirrups, a cool eye, red dots for nostrils, and a long black horsehair tail. When I was little he also had a matching black mane, but my sister gave him a haircut.

This magnificent fellow was made for me during the war. Time weighed heavily on the minds of the air force flight crews my father served with and, to lessen the burden, they would whittle things, repair things, make things, trying to balance out the destruction they were being trained to wreak with small creative acts.

To celebrate my father's new status when I was born, his comrades designed and constructed my marvelous horse, who today stands straight-legged and patient on his red and black wooden base near my bookshelves, still shiny and smiling, waiting for my granddaughter's next visit.

I salvage a few other things: a vase in the shape of a tulip, robin's-egg blue, and a ceramic cat, a Siamese, looking fixedly into a fishbowl—things from my childhood.

When the time comes to choose, my sister takes only things acquired by my mother after we had left home: heavy crystal goblets, silver serving plates, full dinner sets of translucent china. I want only the connection to the past, she wants never to feel it again.

But we aren't there yet, at that time of dispersal of the possessions that tell the story of two lives. Before my horse journeys, secure in his polystyrene peanut bed, to his new home in the company of a Siamese cat and a tulip, several years will pass.

Duuring the Northern Hemisphere summer after my mother's committal I fly again to Canada, swapping the short, snappy Sydney winter for the long expanses of Alberta prairie summer sun that go on forever. At my father's, I stand in the living room at 10:30 in the evening, looking west at the sun setting behind the fir trees, slipping behind the mountains and gilding the pollen and the clouds of tiny insects hanging in the warm air. Everyone else in the house is asleep: my sister, her partner, my father. I stand there dazzled, thinking that I have never felt so alone in my life.

During that visit, a follow-up patient conference is scheduled for my mother at the hospital. My sister doesn't want to go and neither do I but it is compulsory for family, and we are not about to put my father through it.

They tell us that my mother will not attend, presumably since she hijacked proceedings at the previous conference that so bruised my sister. We will represent my father and my father's friend, chosen by her and named in her personal care directive, will be present for her.

I worry we will see her nonetheless, in the hall or in the elevator. It turns out to be worse.

We all wait to file into the conference room: me, my sister, her partner, Dad's friend, the physio, the social worker, the chaplain, the diversional therapist, the ward supervisor, the counselor, and people in scrubs, maybe doctors. We are milling unenthusiastically when the head nurse rounds a corner at speed, pushing my mother in a wheelchair, and cuts in at the head of the line. The wheelchair perplexes me. Isn't she reported to be walking up and down the corridors every day and every night, carrying her walking frame horizontally to poke at people in her way and wearing her Bally pumps?

My sister freezes on the spot in the split second it takes her to see Mum. I fear she may bolt. She wheels around like a horse catching the scent of a bear upwind and I grab her arm. Don't move, I whisper. It's okay.

But it's not. I stand stock-still, holding on to my sister, as my mother is wheeled in first, dressed in black and wearing a somber, wide-brimmed organza hat appropriate for a state funeral, glaring straight ahead of her, with venom but in a general way, deigning to acknowledge no one as she passes before us.

The nurse installs my mother at the head of the table and sits next to her. She places my mother's hand on the table and puts her own over it. We learn later that the nurse has coached my mother: she may attend this meeting, as she has demanded, on condition that she behave. If she begins to cross the line into crazy irrational abusive, as she did at the last conference, the nurse will tap on her hand. If my mother takes no heed and does not dial it down, the nurse will wheel her out. Thus the wheelchair.

My sister and I sit near the opposite end of the long oval table, not facing her. I try to catch her eye. It seems so wrong not to greet her. The one time she looks at me, she stares fixedly with maximum intent. I try to smile and I raise a few fingers. She snorts and turns her head with a vigorous shake to rid herself of me.

Mercifully, I remember little about the conference itself, a slow-motion extrusion of time punctuated by the shuffling of papers, as paraphrase and euphemism and exegesis and repetition suck the oxygen from the air and I sink deeper into a slough of dread and despair.

I know my mother speaks and the head nurse taps on her hand a lot. I don't remember words. Everyone speaks, except my sister, her partner and me. My mother must insist that she does not ever wish to be subjected to visits from family again, although I have no memory of this, because when it is over and my sister and I are standing like stunned mullets in the hallway, trying to process not so much what has gone immediately before but the quaking, liquefying dread we were both flooded with on seeing Mum in battle mode, the chaplain approaches us with what she probably believes are words of comfort.

Your mother will come around, she says. She will want

to see you again. I bite back my reply. I know she won't. I know I have seen my mother for the last time, and this is not the memory I would have liked.

My sister, however, dabs her eyes and says, Thank you. We know she will. And when she does, when that happens, you call us and we'll be here.

I stare at her in amazement. I open my mouth to ask if she is out of her mind, to ask why she would say that. She knows it won't happen. Maybe she is just trying to ingratiate herself with the staff. They will still hate us, I want to yell at her. This woman, this religious person, is the only one speaking to us, you may notice, and only because it's her job.

I'm wrong about nobody else speaking to us, however. The physio comes over to tell us that Mum is still walking a lot, maybe too much, and that she wears her high heels while doing it. We'd be happier, she says, if she wore more appropriate footwear, but we don't want to discourage her from exercising.

My sister amazes me again. She looks the physio earnestly in the eye and I hear her say, Of course not. She goes on. So much has been taken from our mother. We must leave some things up to her. She and the physio nod philosophically.

I wander off toward the elevator, wondering if my sister may harbor a hidden seam of malice which allows her to say these things when I suspect, I am almost sure, that her dearest wish, as it is mine, is for an unfortunate combination of circumstance—a recently mopped floor, impatient speed, and stiletto heels—to put an end to this saga.

Meanwhile, back at the ranch, we settle in for our visit with Dad. My sister's partner repairs the things she can, and she is capable of a lot. The house has been without regular maintenance for a couple of decades and she does all she can, sitting cross-legged on the balcony to reattach the cedar shakes that are working loose from the wall, yipping only mildly when a bat flies directly out at her in response to the taps of her hammer.

She has a go at the bathrooms, but there is no stopping the seeping. I lean on the doorframe and compliment her on her can-do spirit. She tells me good-naturedly that I can wade in anytime and help, but I explain my theory of economic labor distribution. I go to work to make money to pay people to fix bathrooms. She tells me this is all very well and good, but no tradesman will give us the time of day. Every plumber and carpenter and roofer in the area has been out here, once, fixed something and submitted an account, only to have payment refused because my mother wasn't happy with the job, or alternatively to receive a check for twenty-five dollars in the mail with a note saying that this sum is what his work is worth.

We smile. This is banter. She knows I am helping where I can, making dinner and going through dozens of drawers, throwing out scores of old toothbrushes and sorting what I can.

She is kind to me, cutting huge bouquets of lilacs in the garden to put in the living rooms and my bedroom because she knows I love the delicate perfume, the scent of fleeting summer and a reminder of callow youth and first loves.

My sister has given Dad's helpers time off while we are here, and I wish she hadn't. We shower Dad in his en suite where, in spite of recent efforts at repair, the water still runs unpredictably hot and cold. We have to stand outside the shower with the screen open, ready to turn the knobs to adjust the temperature every few seconds, so that he is neither parboiled nor flash-frozen.

One evening I watch my sister as she crouches, trying her best to unplug the shower drain as I man the taps and Dad hunches over, seemingly unaware of how ludicrous this situation is, under the feeble and fickle output of the showerhead, his man gear dangling above my sister's head.

I refrain from shouting at her but I want to.

Here is what I would say. Why can't the helpers work while we are here? How is it our concern that they might need a break? They are used to showering Dad and massaging his feet. Are we trying to save money? He has lots of money. What's it for if not this? Do you want this level of intimacy with Dad, because I sure don't. He's our father, for crying out loud!

I say nothing and watch her stand up, narrowly avoiding a collision of the most inappropriate type, her hair dripping. I send her to dry herself off and I put Dad to bed in his new pajamas, with his pillows plumped up and his quilts piled on because he is always cold, even now, in high summer.

He holds my hand for a moment before I go and gives me his best Paul Newman smile. He shakes his head, as if in wonder, squeezes my hand and says, All that you girls do for me. All that you do.

CHAPTER 22

One year later, I make my last trip to the house on the edge of the foothills. This visit is not tinged with pathos because at the time, as we spend the long sunny days sorting and ferrying Dad to and from the dentist, the podiatrist, the hairdresser, the audiologist, I don't know that I will never see this house again or that it will disappear. I don't know that I will never see this landscape I love from this exact place again.

So I am not sad. This trip feels familiar. We did this last year. We will do it next year.

I have flown to Vancouver from Sydney and rested overnight. We leave in the morning, fresh, and drive east through the lower mainland into the Rockies, up the long incline of the Coquihalla Highway, through the Great Bear Snow Shed that protects the road where it crosses a particularly tricky avalanche run near the Coquihalla Pass at the top.

There are gun turrets along the highway, from which

specialists used to shoot shells into snow on the slopes in winter, creating an avalanche when they wanted it and could close the roads. Now they drop the explosives from helicopters.

This is still one of the most dangerous highways in the world in winter, when an out-of-control semi can material-ize coming sideways at you on black ice, as you clear the top of a steep grade with a rock wall on your left and nowhere to go but down on your right.

In summer, it's different. The road is six lanes wide, the vistas humbling, and we are driving and not flying because I prefer this and said so last year. My sister's partner obliges, driving skillfully for hours through all conditions so that I can see the mountains. This year, I am even braced for the shock of seeing whole slopes of fir trees yellow and dying, victims of the Japanese beetle, an insect that used to be killed off by the brutal cold of a normal winter, never in one season having enough time to damage a tree. With warmer winters, the beetle hunkers down under the bark and endures the cold, surviving to kill its host in the spring. There may be hope. Some species of conifers are more resistant to this bug than others. There is talk of replant-ing, sometime, maybe.

The first night we stop at a motel in Sicamous, House-boat Capital of Canada. The mosquitos are ferocious as it has been uncharacteristically hot and dry this year. The shores of Shuswap Lake have become a marshy paradise for mosquito breeding as the lake shrinks and the water recedes. My sister and I swim in the tiny motel pool and sit a moment in the tiny motel spa, not accompanied by her partner who is from Saskatchewan and does not do water.

Sicamous is a small place, a summer place where the fun is in renting a houseboat and sleeping out on the water. The Trans-Canada Highway bisects it. The lake is on one side and houses and businesses on the other—bait shops, motels, restaurants: Moose Mulligan's, Joe Schmuck's Roadhouse, Bahama John's. At Moose's, I order a lemon, lime, and bitters, and after they question me carefully about what that might be, they do their best and I try to drink some of the result from the milkshake container it comes in, because they tried, that good old Canadian spirit. Over the border in the U.S., they would have just brought me a Sprite.

As we walk in the dark along the highway back to our motel, intermittently deafened by the roar of semis on a tight schedule, I remark to my sister that we are not very visible here on the verge in our dark clothing, that we could be in some danger of being mowed down. I'll fix that, she says, and when the next truck looms ahead of us, she lifts her jumper up to her neck and her white bra shines in the headlights. I don't know if she should be gratified by the long blast of the bullhorn the driver responds with. What if he turns around? I say. Where? she asks. He can't. Has to keep going. She flashes drivers all the way to the motel.

※※

You can drive from Vancouver to Calgary in sixteen hours if you don't stop, but we are taking our time. This is, after all, my holiday for the year, so we think of stopping a second night in a pretentious hotel in a hamlet called Harvie Heights on the eastern slope of the mountains, only because this tiny place is named for our grandfather. He was known as Honest John and I don't think that was ironic. A dour Glaswegian immigrant, he rose through the ranks of the civil service to be deputy minister of lands and mines.

The receptionist in the upmarket mountain-experience lodge announces that she must have two credit card imprints before she will even show us the rooms so we can decide if we really want to spend this much money. As we stare at her, an irate guest interrupts, demanding to know why his room has a fire pit on the patio and instructions for making a fire, but no wood anywhere. She suggests he should climb up the slope behind the hotel and gather some. Bears shouldn't be a problem until dusk. He suggests that he will just break up one of the chairs in his room and burn that.

My sister and I exchange a glance and, as we walk away from Ms. Snarky, we take notebooks and cameras from our bags. We photograph Ms. Snarky from a distance, talking among ourselves about an article and the Canadian Automobile Association. We go outside and stand in a flower-bed to photograph her again through the window, then drive away to find somewhere else to stay.

The next day we spend hours waiting on the highway

behind machines doing roadwork, and we arrive at Dad's several hours later than we expected. My mobile doesn't work and my sister doesn't have hers, so there is no way to let him know we'll be late. He is agitated when we arrive, having worked himself into a lather of worry and annoyance. It's his dementia, the helper whispers to me as we stand in the entrance.

Who said he had dementia? I snap at her.

I don't think he has dementia. Nobody has diagnosed him with dementia. As far as I am concerned, his brain has been working fine since he got off the starvation diet my mother had him on. I think saying he is upset because of his dementia is a convenient way of saying you haven't been bothered to comfort your old charge when he has been worrying himself needlessly into knots.

Maybe I'm wrong. Maybe I should see he's a bit frayed around the edges, especially a week before the end of our stay when he begins fretting at night, wandering the house and counting the money in his wallet, and marking a day off the calendar every morning at breakfast, calculating how many more days we will be there with him. Maybe I should see how disruptive it is for him, how we perturb the rhythm of his days with his carers, the routine he has adapted to since Mum left the house eighteen months ago. He loves that we are there, and when we leave he hates it.

And I don't see the signs with my sister either, even though her feathers are beginning to fall off too. She has been flying here to see Dad every couple of months, sometimes alone and sometimes with her partner, trying to solve all possible problems, trying, I suspect, to predict the unpredictable and control the uncontrollable. After her last visit, when her flight home landed in Vancouver, she stood up to be first off the plane and fainted in the aisle, ensuring that no one could deplane and that her partner had to climb over seats to get to her and the ambulance paramedics, who got on board and blocked the aisle with their gear.

I miss the signs and watch Dad wave goodbye sadly as we leave, thinking we'll come again, having promised him we will.

Life unravels differently. It always does.

Some months later my sister receives a phone call from the agency that has found the helpers for Dad. It is a grim winter's dusk on the coast in Vancouver where she lives, and an evening of robust snowfall and blizzard gales over the Rockies near Okotoks, where Dad is.

The caller informs my sister that the helper on duty today, the big girl we like, the only one we have ever trusted, has just phoned in her resignation from the agency and informed them that she is the only person who has my father's best interests at heart, that his wife is evil and his daughters do not care, that she is with him now and not leaving, and that she will look after him from now on.

He tells my sister he is unsure how to proceed. Never tell my sister you are unsure how to proceed.

She hightails it to the airport and catches the last flight, jouncing around in the snow-clogged air just above the jagged, rocky peaks on blasts of murderous wind. The person who phoned meets her at Calgary airport and they drive through eddying snow, peering through the windscreen as they navigate, very slowly, the blurry, whited-out roads, where the question is not "Are we there yet" but "Are we still on the road," all the way out to my father's place to stage an intervention.

They arrive well after midnight. My sister has keys. The helper is asleep and once roused, expresses surprise at their presence, so strongly does she believe in her mission, the defense of this darling old gentleman, so ill served by the harpies in his life.

I do not know how they arrive at a result, but in the end she packs her things and leaves. She pulls over and waits on the road near the house for some time, but she doesn't come back. My father sleeps through it all.

The next morning, my father asks my sister what she is doing there. He wasn't expecting her. She explains the situation: that she can find new helpers but that the delusional, kleptomaniac, serial killer, drug-addled, gold-digging bunch we've had are the cream of the crop. It can only get worse on that front. The only other solution is that he move to the coast, with her and her partner at first, then somewhere near them in the longer term. She sighs. She hasn't slept and she can't see her way through this. They've spoken of this before. He hasn't wanted to consider it.

He stands up from the breakfast table. Let's go then, he says. But I'll need to bring the cat.

They pack him a bag, turn the water off so the pipes won't freeze, and ask the security company that patrols to double the number of perimeter checks. They put the cat in a blanket in her carry case. As they close the front door, Dad looks back into the great room and says, At least I won't have to look at that damn chandelier anymore.

Here's the problem. You can't leave a big house in the country empty, especially if it has wide windows and is full of things easily sold on to finance an enterprising burglar's needs: the next fix, a payment on a gambling debt.

Word spreads. At best, squatters move in. At worst, pot producers get wind of the opportunity and break in to set up a grow house. Before you know it, and by the time the water and electricity providers flag a huge increase in demand to the house, your abode is a humid ruin and the police are looking at you for production of an illicit substance and maybe trafficking. It is your house, your responsibility.

My sister sets about finding a solution. She learns that our parents' wills are worded so trickily and have been tied in such inextricable knots around the eventual disposal of the property that it is impossible for my father to sell it on his own. My mother has stipulated that the property must go to a land trust, to be protected and maintained the way it is forever, that no money must change hands during this exchange. Even though none of her wishes would hold up under legal scrutiny, we would still need to go to court to challenge them.

Next best solution: we find a renter who is not a drug producer. For this to work, we need to empty the house. My sister calls to see if I will come to Canada. With a team of her friends and her partner, we will live in my father's house for however many weeks it takes to prepare and hold an estate sale, and we will rent the house empty.

I say no. I am still working, but I think I would say no even if I weren't. I see things differently from my sister. She sees a challenge, a showcase for her formidable organizing abilities and perhaps, who knows, a way of dismantling and negating a past that haunts her. I just don't think I owe my parents weeks of backbreaking work and eventual danger. I have ventured only a few feet into the bomb shelter, but what I have seen has discouraged me from ever going further in. I would not send anyone in there without a hazmat suit. I tell her that I will cheer them on from a very great distance.

My sister rises to the logistical occasion. With her partner and six friends, she will travel to Okotoks to sort and clean and donate what is not estate-sale material, and organize what is. In the meantime, her partner's brother will drive up from Medicine Hat and live in the house.

It becomes obvious that for the estate sale to be a success we need to get the word out, and for that we need the help of some estate-sale pros. My sister settles on a company called Estate Sale Pros. They charge a fee for online marketing, and for printing a glossy catalogue and signs and brochures, and for providing a presence on the ground on the day. For a much larger fee, they will take charge of the whole kit and caboodle, the sorting, the cleaning, the discarding, the buffing and polishing and staging. I would have gone that way myself, but my sister moves in with her team to do the prep.

I call them often in the evening, prairie time, when they are exhausted and giddy from whatever they drank at dinner. These are almost all her lifelong friends and I know all but two of them. They take turns telling me funny stories they wish I were there to share. The stories usually end with the idea that maybe you had to be there.

My sister mentions that she seems to be having allergic reactions to something, her tongue tingling, her lips swelling a little, and I reiterate my warnings to stay clear of the bomb shelter and especially the barn. As it turns out, she is not suffering allergies but the first signs of angioedema, an autoimmune condition that will almost kill her some months later, possibly precipitated by fatigue and stress, but we don't know that. I will hear later that she hardly slept for all the weeks the team worked on the house, busy all day and spending part of the night writing up lists of chores for all eight of them for the coming day.

They work every day, no time off, double shifts. They sort, they toss, they cart to the dump, they make lists and separate piles of all manner of things. Two of the team, the ones I do not know, will not go the distance. They complain about the living arrangements, the food, and the chores they are assigned. They don't ferry bottles and cans to the dump but take them to another town altogether to cash them in, and keep the proceeds. When they are evicted, they pay themselves for their trouble by secreting a number of objects in their bags, as a salve to the battler's resentment they feel toward the well-to-do.

The magnificent six push bravely forward each day after this setback. My sister's brother-in-law takes on the barn. He removes toxic chemicals dating back to before the concept of toxic chemicals. He repairs mowers and refurbishes a cutter sleigh nobody knew was there, and a cast iron horse-head hitching post.

Even though it is late in the spring and the crab apple trees have bloomed, they are snowed in twice. The second blizzard is a momentous storm. If my father had still lived there when it hit, he would have died. The electricity is cut off, so there is no heat as the furnaces won't light. The team sleeps in their outdoor gear and boots.

There is no water, as the pumps for the well run on electricity. They can't flush the toilets. They cook under a tarp on a barbecue in a sheltered corner of a patio and melt snow for water to drink. They all want a shower. They can't get out. The roads are blocked for miles around.

After a couple of days, when the snow melts, you can see the tiny green shoots of crocuses piercing up through the ground, looking for light, having another go at announcing spring. The roads open. The Estate Sale Pros arrive in their SUVs to make lists for the catalogue and to take pictures.

It will be seventeen pages long, photos and text, inviting prospective buyers to "see this home and homestead, full of the most amazing antiques ever offered for sale in one estate."

The text is breathless and features a number of crimes against quotation marks ("very desirable grandfather clock"), and some juxtapositions I would find funny if the whole business weren't breaking my heart. One reads on the first page that "this is a 4800 sq. ft. home packed full of antique treasures and modern small appliances," and under the photo of my mother's antique dining room buffet ("amazing"), the caption spells it out: "attached scrollwork mirror supports, cutlery drawer, four cathedral-topped cupboard doors with matched panels of glorious burl veneer. Dating to the late 1800s, this is definately [sic] a showpiece in any home."

So far, so good. But since this is the Wild West, the author can't help but conclude, "Try to imagine it as a bar in a party room."

My sister and the team hold a presale event for family and neighbors. My parents' entire life is laid out on trestle tables by category, with a price on every object. My cousin David buys several dozen bottles of good Bordeaux from my father's cellar, Ducru-Beaucaillou 1972. My former husband took my father to visit that château which belonged to family friends, and I can see him in my mind's eye, loving every minute in the cellars, talking to the owners. I wish he had drunk his wine, but since he didn't, I'm glad my cousin will.

The day after the presale event, one of my sister's team, a big jovial man with white hair and a beard, drives into Okotoks and, looking like a Santa Claus recruited into the Hells Angels, deposits the proceeds of the evening into my father's account, under the worried and suspicious stare of the locals.

The main event takes place over the following weekend, May 13 to 15. What should be ample parking festooned in a field soon overflows as hundreds of people come to troll through the house, to snoop and haggle and to buy, following the directions in the brochure for getting to the property: "Leave Calgary going south on the Deerfoot Trail towards Fort MacLeod. Take the 2A turnoff to the right, towards Okotoks. At the top of the first hill, there is a radio tower on the right and a horse arena on the left. You will be turning right here, past a house with corrals and a large red barn, and continuing to a T-junction." I can see it all in my mind as I read.

At this point, what the prospective buyers see is what I saw every time I came here. They see a parkland of clipped lawns, weeping willows with pale tendrils stirring in the breeze, and stands of conifers. What they also see, however, and what I have been lucky not to see, is a house with doors wide open, people with clipboards in matching vests inviting them in to pick through the remains of what can only be known and understood in context; to contribute, as vultures do in the desert, to the dispersal of the vestiges of life.

CHAPTER 24

Dad settles into a new routine on the coast at my sister's. The house is large and square, on a big flat block of land. It is a functioning bed-and-breakfast, and was the first brick in the now impressive wall of properties owned and managed by my sister and her partner. Having my father there presents no physical problem. A couple of new handrails do the trick, and he is at home in the Rose Room: a comfortable double bed, an en suite of hospital-grade cleanliness and, through the weeping willow branches that sweep gently across the wide window, a view to a quiet suburban street, no footpaths, clipped lawns, people walking and cycling and exercising their dogs in the early morning mist on the shiny surface of the road, sparkling like wet coal after the most recent shower.

My sister says her suburb is working-class; she also tells me that she considers herself working-class. When I stop laughing and ask for her definition of this, she says, Working-class—working, having a job. Dictionary in hand, I endeavor to explain that while that may be definition number three or four, the usual meaning has to do with other concepts: white-collar or blue-collar; propertied or landless; education or lack thereof; dependence on the sweat of your brow to put food on the table for the kids, or having a savings account, a trust fund, a safety net. I mention Dickens and Austen. I complicate things by bringing in the rural poor.

She won't budge. I explain that by her definition Australian mining magnate Gina Rinehart is working-class. She doesn't know who that is and I don't know who the Canadian equivalent would be. I say that if her neighbors were a working-class family of four, they wouldn't have two cars and an RV parked in the drive. I try to make her see that we have sprung desperately from a violently aspirational upper-middle-class background, and that I see that as part of the greater malaise we live with. She just shakes her head and repeats, working-class.

So, in his new working-class suburb, my relentlessly cheerful father adjusts seamlessly, goes for little walks and drives my sister batty by asking brightly at breakfast, So what are we doing today? He is always up for a car ride to the bank or to the low-rise apartment block where their furnished rental units are.

My sister adapts with more difficulty to the realities of always traveling with an offsider in his nineties. She is used to moving fast and multitasking, and she runs head-on into the same equation new mothers must learn to solve: you only go as fast as the slowest member in your wagon train.

She is in agony, transferring items off her list of goals to be met that day and onto tomorrow's list, weaning herself off her reliance on speedy outcomes. She idles at the curb a lot.

I have foreseen this.

Once my mother was safely institutionalized, not to be released, and Dad was snugly ensconced on his property with round-the-clock care, such as it was, I told my sister that anything more we would do for our father was icing on the cake. We could now walk away and not be involved in his day-to-day issues; we could leave all this to the friend who holds the power, the stranger chosen by our parents to decide upon their care as they decline. However badly we might predict that this would all play out, we could just visit Dad at Christmas.

I reminded her that Dad went along with my mother in disinheriting us, and removing any right we had to help him in his old age; that, most hurtfully of all, he believed everything she told him about us, even though he now holds other views. It is as a result of his own inability to act that he now barely has a connection with us and has none whatsoever with his grandchildren.

I have often said all this and most recently, when she changed his documents to name her as carer, carried out the intervention and brought him to Vancouver, I told her bluntly, Do not do this. Not unless you can carry it alone, because I am not here, and I can't be here every time there is a problem. You will be alone with this, and your partner will have to deal with this, and I can see sinkholes of simmering resentment about to develop between us.

But we came when the call went out for help that cold December day almost three years ago, and we really can't stop now. Everything I say to her, I say to myself, and I don't convince either of us. I know that neither of us can walk away from him, and that my sister's taking my father in may spell the end of her relationship with me, because she will hate me for not doing half of the hard work. I can't fix this.

My father can, however.

My sister and her partner are preparing for their yearly vacation in Hawaii two months after Dad moves in with them. They have told him from the beginning that they will be going away for six weeks in late winter, and that they have rented a nice unit for him to stay in while they are away. The unit is in a third-age complex called Pacific Peace, a nonprofit golden-years operation with "assisted living" and nursing home facilities. Eagles soar above the oak grove out the back.

My father has a two-bedroom Timberwolf suite, bigger than the Lynx or the Coyote, and named for a mountain dweller never seen this close to the coast. My sister arranges for private registered nurses to be with him every waking hour and administer insulin to his diabetic cat.

He walks in the manicured grounds with his companions and sits in the pergola watching the squirrels bound across the dewy grass and up the trunks of trees. He refuses most company at his table in the dining room, only tolerating Gerta, who came to Canada from northern Europe years ago and has an accent as weighty as her stolid self. She is a tough and reliably critical woman given to believing the worst about everything and everyone, with some excuse, as rumor has it that she is only here under severe duress.

She was a woman on the land and comes to Pacific Peace with her cat, Stig, a lively farmworker himself. Stig kills various small things outside and drags them into the foyer, eliciting the ire of the director, a woman named Rosemary. My sister and I will decide that Gerta fills a void for Dad, the empty space reserved for a carping, deluded woman who will endlessly remind him to be wary of everyone around him.

When my sister and her partner return from Hawaii, the last thing they are expecting is what Dad announces. He has decided not to return to their house, but to stay on at this very pleasant place, in his airy and spacious suite with a view across the road to the potato fields, where the weightless white blossoms are just appearing on the plants.

He says he might even buy the place, by which he means not just his unit but the whole complex: the park and the trees, the eagles in the air, the coaches that take residents on scenic drives and the coordinated pastel sofas and armchairs in the common area, the elevators and the nice people who come to remind him when to take his meds.

When I arrive two months later to visit, I find him

contentedly talking to Gerta, conversations that usually begin with: Do you have any idea how much I'm worth? I join them for meals, and Gerta brings me up to speed on what Dad eats and does not eat. She is big, protective, and abrasive, her slate-gray hair cut in a bob with a fringe, like the little Dutch boy who put his finger in the dike in the folk tale. I look at all the pleasant women at other tables. The ratio of women to men is about fifty to one. I take in their pearl earrings and their twinsets, their pastel canes and animated conversations among themselves, their still graceful gestures and the wistful gazes they sometimes slide my father's way, and I marvel at the complexities of the human heart. He chose Gerta.

He looks shrewdly at me during a lull in the conversation and then asks me if I know how much he's worth. I reply that no one does really, and he's off and running.

There is something wrong with my sister. I know this when I get off the plane for this visit. I arrive at 7:40 a.m. the day before I left Sydney, this sixteen-hour nonstop flight from Australia having crossed the date line and landed on time, as usual. What is not usual is that my sister is not where she always is to pick me up. I wait and she arrives an hour later, flustered, and tells me that she decided on a whim to test her blood sugar this morning before coming to get me. As a prediabetic in a holding pattern, she is supposed to do this every month or so. She hasn't been doing it.

This morning her reading is off the charts and she is going to the hospital as soon as she drops me home. I take a nap, and when I wake, my sister probably explains to me what is going on with her, what they recommended at the hospital, but my jet-jangled brain does not transfer this to memory. I cannot now recall what she said.

What I do remember is that after dinner that evening, my sister complains that her tongue is a bit swollen, something that happened several times when she was on our parents' property with her friends months earlier, when they were getting ready for the estate sale. She takes an antihistamine and we all go to bed.

Her partner wakes me an hour later, bursting into my room to tell me to throw on some clothes if I want to go to the hospital with them. My sister is already in the car when I stumble into the carport seconds later, her partner at the wheel, backing out of the drive while I am still climbing into the back seat. My sister is unrecognizable, her eyes slits in her swollen face, her breath rasping as she struggles for air, her hands batting at her throat. Her partner guns it down the sleeping street, slows slightly at the red light at a main intersection before speeding straight across the six deserted lanes against the light. At the hospital, we leave the car in the ambulance bay with the doors open and help my sister stagger into Emergency.

She worked in hospitals all her adult life. She knows the drill. She collapses on the admissions desk and people surround her, coming out of nowhere, carrying her through the swinging doors into a place of flashing lights and tubes and monitors, blocking me and her partner and shouting that we cannot follow, that we need to go sit on the blue plastic chairs in the waiting area.

We do. We sit down in the sudden silence with all the other people who stare and then turn their eyes away, relieved that whatever is happening to them is nowhere near as bad as what they have just seen. I drink some water as my sister's partner goes out to move the car.

Then we wait.

When they let us into the emergency ward to see my sister, she is sitting propped up in the bed, drooling. She can't swallow and her tongue is so swollen she cannot talk. She is communicating by gesture and grunt that she needs a suction tube to deal with the dribbling. She is as wall-eyed as a horse trapped in a canyon, jittery and terrified, but she's still trying to take charge.

Above her head, the monitors pop and ping incessantly. Blood pressure alert, heart rate alert. And yet they keep putting the nebulizer mask on her to administer more steroids, elevating those readings further each time. She keeps tearing the mask off, and she's right.

They think she is in anaphylactic shock due to an allergy, and you give steroids for that. The trouble is that this isn't working, so they give her more of them. The monitors are trying to tell us that she will stroke out or arrest if this goes on. Her partner, who was for decades a medical person herself, is speaking quietly but with some urgency to the people around us. She keeps her own counsel at all times, but I read concern in the tight set of her shoulders, the short, sharp way she is moving her hands as she talks.

Nobody knows what my sister has, but it's looking less like anaphylaxis by the minute. In fact she has angioedema, and the emergency doctors could conceivably kill her by treating her for allergy, but they cannot know this. They are the first responders, whose job it is to keep her alive. They treat what they see and if it is quacking like a duck, they can only deem it a duck.

I sit next to my sister, not even considering that this might worsen and end here, not knowing that the statistics show you have only a 48 percent chance of surviving this kind of attack. I am solid in a faith firmly rooted in the viewing of medical drama on TV that the people working here are heroes. No one makes mistakes and nobody dies. This allows me to sit quietly beside her, patting her leg under the sheet.

Sometime before dawn she improves. They send us home and will summon us later to pick her up, after they have observed her for a while.

She comes home later that day looking normal, with no idea why she came so near to not making it and afflicted with a textbook case of what newspapers, when reporting the mad and murderous behavior of bouncers in clubs or meltdowns in gyms and on sporting fields, refer to as "'roid rage." She is hyped-up, so high on steroids that her feet barely graze the ground. She is in perpetual motion and carries on a nonstop, animated dialogue with her inner crazy person. It will take days for this to wear off.

She goes off at her partner, at me, at the friends staying with us, like a cluster bomb: a flash of sulfur igniting, words she cannot take back delivered with such force and conviction that you have to believe she means at least some of them. In this state she has done nothing to bring upon herself, part of my sister's keen distress must result from her registering what she is doing, and hearing what she is saying.

Her need for movement means that the dog gets a lot of walks. I accompany her to stride around the running track at the local high school and she explains to me that we need to plan out the rest of my stay. We need some goals, steps to get there. I plan to survive if possible. That is my goal. I do not say this.

What I do say is that I would like to see my father every day but beyond that, we can do whatever she likes.

Wrong answer.

No, she shouts. No, no, no! She throws the doggie bag of poo on the ground. She stamps her feet in a frenzy. No, no, no, she tells me. That is not how it has to work. He should not get back better than he put in. You come here to see him, in spite of what he did and didn't do. I practically have to die to get your attention.

I will not forget my dismay at hearing what she says, but I will only be pushed so far. I insist that I will see Dad every day.

We stomp back home and the following days pass in a state of uneasy truce, me getting taken to task for caring more about getting my laundry done than spending time with her, for preferring to browse in a children's shop for my granddaughter while she and a friend go look at homewares. I don't even know what those are.

I try my best. We all do. She becomes gradually less livid but remains dictatorial. At breakfast the day of a barbecue she has refused to cancel on the pretext that we can all just pitch in and it will be fine, she circulates a list of chores to be accomplished for the barbecue to be a success.

We are to pass it around the breakfast table and, at each passage, put our initial after a task we choose until there are none left. I choose "Cut tomatoes for salad," initial that item and pass it on. My second choice is "Put greens in salad bowl." At the third passage I can't help myself and, straight-faced, suggest that I don't think I can do more. My sister looks solemnly at me and says that of course she does not expect anyone to commit to more than he or she can do. I honestly can't tell if she's having me on.

Later, as we prepare in the kitchen, I whisper to my sister's friend that she has to cover for me because I need to go get my dad. She will have to do my two initialed tasks for me. I don't want to talk to my sister about it. The friend gives me a you-need-a-hug look but she is holding a potato peeler and just nods sympathetically.

It's just the drugs talking, I tell her. I know this. Still, I start counting the days until I leave like an insomniac counts sheep, hoping she won't relapse in the interim.

At the barbecue, I hear the fellow who was our host at Christmas talking to my sister about steroids. He says, I know, I know. You listen to yourself saying these things to the people you love. You hear what you are saying and yet you can't stop yourself.

She gets better. We walk the dog at the park where her friends, all owners of Labradors, assemble. The dogs play well together, most are well trained, and I'm happy to be out in the air with everybody until the day of the dogfight.

A new dog, who is being looked after by one of the Labrador owners, has been added to the mix. He's a working dog, a mongrel, scrappy and rangy. His interest is in herding everybody, and he circles the canines and the humans, nudging and nipping to get everyone rounded up. I cringe as he bangs into the back of my knees, the dog owners yell, frenzied barking breaks out, and I am nearly bowled over by rolling, roiling masses of dog.

My sister steps in front of me, pushes me back against the wall of the toilet block, and says, Don't move. Then she wades out into the dogs to sort things out.

I don't think I told her afterward how proud I was of her, how safe I felt. I did, however, tell her that I wouldn't go to the dog park again, but I would go to cat parks if she knew the whereabouts of any. She was delighted with this comment and relayed it to her dog-owner friends.

※

When I visit my father, he reminisces. He says, Do you remember the time . . . ? I don't, because usually I wasn't born. I say, Tell me about that again, Dad, and he does.

But something in his brain has stretched and snapped like an old elastic band. Whatever kept his grip on reality firm and his strong autocensor in place is dissolving, and disparate things are spilling out. I'm getting Dad 2.0, director's cut. When I invite him to tell me about that again, I'm expecting more tales of financial derring-do and how much he's worth, but there is a change.

I am hearing stories of single-engine planes over the jungle, of being spirited out the back door of bodegas where he was eating by minders who hide him under a canvas in the bottom of a pirogue and paddle him down the river to safety. There are tales of women, important and influential women but damsels in distress nonetheless, snatched out of harm's way by his courage.

I know that after he retired from a big oil company when he was sixty, he set up his own one-man petroleum consultancy firm with my mother as codirector. I always presumed that he did this to be able to claim some of her extravagances against tax.

He did go to dangerous places for clients. He was in Pakistan when Ali Bhutto was executed in 1979, and stopped over in France with us on his way home. I've seen the Colombian stamps in his old passport. I don't believe everything in the stories he's telling me, but there may be truth there. I have no clue what he did in those places.

After dinner at the retirement home, I watch him fold

his napkin next to his plate and lean back in his chair, doing what people have done forever around fires in caves and at kitchen tables and over lavish place settings at gala fundraisers—settling in to yarn and embellish, to tell the stories of who we are or who we think we are.

He interrupts the flow of the narrative and looks around to see if anyone can hear, then leans across the table and says, like a conspirator, But when she saw the size of my penis, she just backed away and said, Oh, no. No, no. He smiles to himself.

I stare into my coffee cup, resisting the urge to put my hands over my ears and chant la-la-la-la-la. I have seen my father in the shower and have no doubt that he was a fine figure of a man when he was younger, but I need more resilience than I have right now to deal with so much too much information. I take my leave and walk around in the little communal garden outside as I wait for my sister to pick me up. The asters are blooming. I study the asters.

I get into the car with her and tell her about the misfirings in Dad's head. I tell her about the lady's backing away and about her comment. My sister has to pull the car over because we are laughing until the tears run down our faces, and the tears keep coming for quite some time.

At the airport when I'm leaving, my sister, who is now acting completely normal, looks worried and says, Was I very mean to you?

I tell her it was the drugs talking.

My sister's life is difficult. She is afraid of another attack, afraid she will die if she has one. She is terrified of going into hospital, into that environment where for years she worked and felt in supreme control, making the best possible decisions for other people, and where she now finds herself just another patient. Worse—a patient they don't know how to help. She doesn't like what her life looks like from here on. It makes her testy.

She is dozy from antihistamines; she complains of feeling fuzzy and not being herself when it comes to multitasking. I tell her nobody ever multitasked like her, that if she is even half of what she was, she's still ahead of us all.

She does research, calls in favors from doctor friends to get new opinions. She learns that there is congenital angioedema and acquired. She has the second. This knowledge is of no help, as nobody knows how to prevent attacks or treat either one effectively.

The attacks have a trigger, they must, so she follows an elimination diet, just in case. She can have pears and rice. Maybe fish. Meat is fine. No shellfish, potatoes or tomatoes or spinach. No spices or nuts or additives, colors, preservatives. No commercially prepared food. No airplane food.

She and her partner, who are in the habit of eating out every day, socializing in restaurants with their friends, and traveling, now bake their own bread and eat plain at home.

When I call, I don't probe but I ask how she is. I listen to details of tests, my head awash with acronyms I have never heard, trying hard to comprehend the hypotheses of the week. What I actually retain is that nobody has a clue. She lists what she can and cannot do, and I vehemently wish that she wasn't suffering constraints on all sides as soon as she wakes up.

She is convinced that the weeks spent whipping my parents' house into shape with her friends, in preparation for the estate sale, exposed her to toxins that are at the root of her problem. I'm sure she was exposed to toxins but I think they may have been more psychological than physical, as she busied herself in our mother's space, dismantling our mother's life. Maybe she senses this underneath. She is adamant she can't talk about our parents, as it upsets her.

She is sure stress is a trigger. She drops into the conversation that when her GP asked what stress she had been under before the attack I was present for, she mentions my arrival for a visit. My silence must alert her to a possible stress on my end of the telephone line, because she adds defensively, A good stress of course, but a stress nonetheless.

I listen. She is my sister and I care about her. She's sick. She is my link to my father. I listen.

Our conversations end abruptly. She tells me suddenly that she doesn't want to talk about all of this. The next time we speak, she wants to talk about something else. She hangs up.

I want to talk about other things too. I want her to ask how I am. I want to know how her partner is faring, off in the kitchen, kneading. I want news of Dad, because when I phone him he is never wearing his hearing aid or it isn't working and all I get are generic remarks.

It's good to hear your voice, he says, which I know is code for I can't hear anything at all.

How's the weather where you are? he asks, a Canadian conversational staple. You can't go wrong with that one. I tell him. Drought and bush fires, tornadoes and waterspouts, torrential rains and flooded lawns alive with funnel-web spiders, wolf spiders, trapdoor spiders, all water-skiing at speed from their muddy burrows toward drier ground in my garage, where I await them with my ladies' gardening spade. That's good, he says, after what seems to him a suitable pause.

And everyone is fine in your neck of the woods? Yes, I answer. Everyone in my neck of the woods is dandy. I can't even contemplate telling him the truth, although when I think about it, I could. I could tell him all manner of appalling things, and after another calibrated pause he would just say, That's nice, I'm glad.

Over time, my sister's health stabilizes, and my father's declines gently. I am the mobile one, so I go to visit.

Dad has now left his airy, self-care two-bedroom apartment for a large studio with en suite in a separate part of the complex. There are twelve studios arranged around a spacious living area with tropical fish, a piano, overstuffed upholstered furniture and a huge flat-screen television. There is a dining room and a walled garden to walk in. This part of the complex is called Halcyon House.

The director has been urging this move upon us for some time, saying that my father will benefit from the constant care available, that of course he can bring his cat, that it is time.

I don't believe a word. I don't think it's time. I think she needs his apartment for somebody else. I resisted her last efforts to instigate this move.

It does seem to make sense to downsize now, however, instead of hiring private nurses to live with him in a roomy flat where he has never even sat on the balcony, and where he wears a path in the carpet from bathroom to bedroom to his favorite chair in the living room while his carer does sudoku. The director has pushed hard this time, urging us to take advantage of an unexpected vacancy, the pleasantest of the studios, with large windows and good light. This may not be available again.

I feel it would be a downer to call to her attention that this studio will be available again. This place is the last stop before the end of the line. You may be able to climb down from your carriage and stroll the platform, sit for a while on a bench in the sun watching the swoop and glide of the eagles flying high above their nest in the tallest oak, but you will get back on the train to complete your journey. The next vacancy is never far away.

So where he lives now is a place with a locked door that opens with a code. As she is selling the move to us, the director emphasizes that this is a higher-care option and definitely, absolutely, and totally not a dementia unit, although people with evolving cognitive difficulties can safely dwell there. Dad can have the code and come and go as he wishes.

He goes along with the idea and I hear that the move goes smoothly. My sister takes him out to lunch while her partner and some helpers move his furniture. He returns midafternoon to nap in a new place and they all go home exhausted to lie down.

He takes change like a trouper. When the health of his old cat fails, he discusses the options with my sister and concludes, reasonably and sadly, that it wouldn't be right to try to keep her going any longer. He is calm and sits with the cat before my sister puts her in her carry case to go to the vet's. But he doesn't get out of bed the next morning, or the next, or the next. And in this higher-care facility, where my father's standard of care does not look to me to be improving, they do end up noticing.

My sister and her partner go to the animal rescue shelters and find Calico II, another female, not as portly as the pet my father is grieving and with a rat-bag personality of tiger proportions quite unlike the other's, but outwardly similar to Calico I. They take her to my father, who gets out of bed to look after her and help her settle in.

For a while, he keeps her jealously to himself, always asking us, when we leave his studio with him, to check that she is inside. The cat is, of course, craftier than anyone in the place and is soon feted at every table in the dining room at mealtimes. After a season or two, my father decides that he could let her go outside into the walled garden in the daytime. Unimpressed by walls, she goes over or under or through, makes friends with the priest of the parish in the church next door and invites his cat over to Dad's for snacks and sleepovers.

When I visit, I see Dad declining in tiny increments. He is almost the way I saw him months before on my last visit: just a little stiffer, a little slower, a little deafer. He feels the downward slide though. He tells my sister he needs to contact the Royal Canadian Air Force to tell them that something has happened to his body. He feels that it is probably the result of his wartime experiences and he thinks they should know about it. He'd like some answers.

My sister suggests that he can hardly sue the air force for premature aging or untimely demise, given his age. He agrees and says that he doesn't need the money anyhow.

We wonder if he is losing it when one day he tells us that he cannot find the clock with the luminescent dial that is always on his night table. He says he woke in the night and, reaching for it, encountered the hand of someone standing there, stealing his clock.

My sister and I look at each other. She crawls under the bed and finds the clock cushioned in wreaths of six-month-old dust. My dad insists. I grabbed someone's wrist, he says. There was someone in here.

He is telling the truth. The stylish lady in the studio next to him has taken to roaming at night, convinced that she needs to get dressed since someone is coming to pick her up and take her home. The staff are invisible, and since none of the studios lock, she opens doors, looking for help. She absentmindedly picks things up as she goes and puts them down elsewhere. Dad must have given her a fright when he grabbed her wrist.

She is partial to Dad's room because she loves the cat.

As she sinks into confusion and incomprehension, and leaves her room less often, the cat begins to go to her. When you glance into her room, you see this lady lying stiffly on the bed so that she won't crease her outfit, as well turned out as ever in her pantsuits and blazers and pearls, one arm curled around Dad's cat, asleep beside her. In company of the cat, she waits patiently, as do most here, for people who never come.

My father gazes mildly upon this lady, upon the fellow who professes effusively, every day of the week, that he is so pleased to finally meet us, upon the grinch who gives the waitresses serious grief every meal about the temperature of the food, and upon the staff, holed up in the nurses' station. He says, Do you ever get the feeling that you and I are the only sane ones in here?

My sister answers, All crazy except thee and me.

They finish the joke in unison: And I'm not too sure about thee.

M y mother's death takes me by surprise. It feels sudden and unexpected, against all logic, in spite of her great age. I haven't been expecting her to bury us all, as the saying goes, because I'm pretty sure she wouldn't bother, but I have expected her to outlive us. In my mind, she has remained indomitable, cast in bronze.

We are warned. Dad's friend informs us three days before that she has taken to her bed and is not eating. The staff believe the end is nigh. My sister, from Hawaii, questions him about how nigh is nigh, and wants an estimated time frame. I don't know why, because neither of us is rushing to be there. We cannot legally get in to see her. We can't even phone the hospital for news.

My mother goes peacefully in her sleep, against all odds. If anyone was going to rage against the dying of the light, I would have put my money on her. She has beside her a companion person hired many months ago to aerate her self-imposed solitude, so she does not die alone. I find this comforting.

My sister keeps me posted about how she is. I thought I would feel happier, she says. Why? I ask. After a few days she tells me that, while she has sad moments when she thinks of good things about Mum, she is now back to her normal self. Laughing and functional, she says.

I look in the mirror. I say Ho-ho-ho to myself, just to try it out. My reflection shrugs. I'm functional though. I have that.

We begin to disagree about telling Dad. As long as my sister is in Hawaii, we agree he won't be told. Neither of us wants a casual care worker with limited English to break the news between mopping and swabbing.

Once my sister is back in Vancouver, I bring the issue up again. She thinks he doesn't need to know. She tells me she will just follow his lead. If he asks for news of Mum, she will say, What would you like to know? Ask me what you want to know and if I can tell you anything, I will.

How often has he brought her up in the last years? I ask.

That's what I'm saying, my sister says. Once, maybe twice. He's erased her from his life. It would just upset him to know. He might get confused. He might think you died.

She feels she knows all of this, but who ever knows what is in someone else's heart? Who is even sure what is in her own?

I am diplomatic in expressing my distress at her position though, because she could just tell me that if I think I know best, I should get myself on an airplane to Canada and participate in the process.

So I say I'm not completely comfortable with not telling him. I say it isn't ours to decide, that I would feel angry and betrayed if people who thought they knew best kept something important from me just because I was old. I say, How would you feel?

I tell her that I feel differently about Mum's story now that the last page has been written. Only a bit. It's subtle, nothing dramatic, but the difference is there. Dad should be allowed to feel this too. What would give us the right to decide he shouldn't? I bring myself to use the word "closure."

I trot out the clincher. What, I say, if he gets a condolence card from somebody and we haven't told him? What if he finds out that way? What if someone phones? Why would he ever trust us again?

He won't find out like that, she says. Nobody will know she's died and he has no contact with anyone in Alberta. Who would write to him? And anyhow, I'm having his mail held until I can look at it.

It's his mail, I say. That's illegal.

She trots out her clincher. Dad is happy to let her look after things. Here's an example, she says. We bought him a new coat. The lining wasn't attached properly. He saw me repairing it and asked what I was doing. I explained and he was happy to let me repair the coat.

Has he had the coat for over seven decades? I ask. Has it made his life hell and nearly ruined him as well as giving him, we hope, the happiest moments of his life? Has he put his feelings for the coat deep in his chest so that they won't inconvenience anyone, and won't hurt so much?

The next morning I get an email from a former neighbor of my father's in the foothills. She tells me she is sorry to hear of my mother's death, as are all the other neighbors who knew my parents. She asks if I could confirm Dad's address so she can send him a card. She tells me how she heard. A woman who moved from the area a few years ago has kept an eagle eye on Okotoks, its environs and inhabitants, by trawling the websites of the town halls, the retirement homes, the hospitals and funeral parlors. Even though Mum specifically requested no funeral and no notices in the press, this woman knows and has alerted everyone. I forward the email to my sister.

She and her partner speak to the director of Pacific Peace and ask her advice. She tells them that she has seen families go both ways, either keeping the secret of a loved one's death from an old frail person, or sharing the news. Hoping to keep this secret is, in her words, a recipe for disaster.

My sister's partner prints a recent photo of my mother, sent to us by Dad's friend when he wrote to tell us she was gone. On the back, she writes my mother's full name, her date of birth and the date of her death. She goes with my sister to see Dad, and they break the news. He seems to understand. He smiles sadly as he looks at the photo. She was a nice gal, he says eventually. Never had children though.

He lifts his head after this last remark, and looks at my sister. He adds, Except for you and your sister, of course.

My sister's partner writes to me. She says that it is sometimes hard to gauge exactly what is going on in my father's mind. And if I am honest, I have seen him in moments of blankness, when a fog seems to encroach. In those moments, there is no panic in him, no anger. It looks almost comforting, like the fog rolling in over the bay to blanket San Francisco, filling in the awkward spaces and leveling everything, cottony and soft, feathers or fairy floss. Every time I see him, I tell myself that there aren't many of those moments, and that you can't begrudge a person of his age a few minutes of confusion once in a while.

I don't want him to go. I want him to know me the next time I see him.

And he probably will. He tells my sister he is frustrated living in a place with goofy people who don't know what is going on. He asks my sister if he is in the right place. She explains that he is but that unfortunately there are confused people with nowhere to be, so they have to live where he is for the moment.

She says, I know it is frustrating for you. Is there any-thing I can do to help? He shakes his head. No, he says. She asks if he would like to take a minute before giving such a definitive answer. He smiles at her and shakes his head. No, he says.

I look into my own future, perhaps not that far off, when I will be aware of banks of fog on the horizon, coming my way. I think of a world where people will have emails delivered directly onto a permanent contact lens, scanning content as they walk, a discreet pinging noise in their frontal lobes alerting them to new communications. A world where supermodels Photoshopped in the flesh and wearing outlandish underwear, with feathered wings attached to their shoulder blades, stalk the streets in small flocks, teetering awkwardly on five-inch heels like adolescent giraffes. A world where Canada is no longer on any map, because of what the U.S. calls, after a short and surprisingly bloody period of "readjustment," the 49th Parallel Energy Rationalization Impetus, and what the Canadian underground fighters, the few who are left, call the Great Water Wars, or the Oil Sand Wars, or the Fracking Wars.

Bring on the fog, I say.

When I speak to my father on Skype at Christmas, he is silent. He looks at me as I talk to him, my sister and her partner hovering in the background, and he smiles. He looks pleased but he doesn't speak. Days later, when I tell my sister how sad I was that he didn't know me, she tells me I have it all wrong. They talked about it afterward, and he was amazed to see me so clearly.

When my sister asks him why he didn't respond or answer my questions, why he was silent, he scoffs. She was on TV, he says. I was watching her on TV. Who talks to a TV set? That would be crazy.

※

Just off Highway 7, six miles southwest of Okotoks, my mother's spirit sits on the edge of the huge *V*-shaped boulder cracked down the middle, known as the Okotoks Erratic, and dangles her feet above the thirty-foot drop. She is wearing her ankle-length black mink coat and matching hat, and French high-heeled pumps. She looks up at the flawless sky, the millions of stars, the tiniest sliver of a moon, all that blackness.

Napi, the Blackfoot trickster character, swoops in like a snowboarder, his buffalo-skin cloak flying, and sits next to her, showering her with ice crystals.

Nice hat, he says. She nods, looking at her shoes which, she is just realizing with horror, are made of calfskin.

The hat's mink, she says. Farmed mink. Sorry.

Nobody's perfect, he says. And you did choose a really cold night for it. It's brass monkeys out here. You need something warm to wear.

And as the northern lights begin to drift across the sky, mauve and aqua and leaf-green, he tells her the story of his cloak.

One hot day, he stopped to rest on this very rock. He spread his cloak out and lay down. When he was refreshed, he left his cloak as a token of thanks to the rock for its hospitality. But he hadn't gone many miles before the rain set in and he returned to the Okatok, which is what the rock is called in the Blackfoot language, to take his cloak back.

The Okatok was furious, and as Napi ran across the foothills, clutching his cloak, the rock chased him, rolling faster and faster, picking up tremendous speed. All Napi's friends—the elk, the deer, the bear, the coyotes and the prairie dogs—tried to help by running between him and the rampaging rock to slow it down, but they were crushed by its huge weight.

The Okatok was gaining on Napi. His friends the bats were his last chance. They saw a fault line in the rock from above. They took turns diving and diving, hitting the fault line, their little faces getting flatter after every hit, a physical trait of these bats that remains to this day. Finally, a thunderous crack echoed in the sky as the rock broke in two and came to a halt where it lies today.

So, he concludes, watching the curtains of color sweep across the sky, don't apologize for the mink. We do what we can. You protected the animals on your property. You didn't let the white guys come there and kill for fun. And remember that first day, when you went for a drive around your new place and you found that badger on the side of the road, its back broken, hit by a car, just lying there panting? I saw you go to the nearest house and get the rancher to come with his rifle to put it out of its misery. You had to insist. You did good.

My mother's spirit is pleased, but then he adds, You might not know, but your daughters try to do good too.

I don't have children, she says.

Can't trick the Trickster, he says. And were you even listening to the story about my cloak? It's about not taking back what you have given.

Your daughters, he continues, holding up a finger to silence her, should you have had any, try too. One of them raises money for the Pacific Whale Foundation. The other one signs things. Don't cull the sharks. Stop live animal exports. It doesn't do much good, but it's something.

The aurora borealis is fading. Well, he says, show's over. Gotta see a man about a dog. You should move on too. You'll have more scope now, for the good stuff.

He waves his arm. Wider view, he says. Farther reach. But only for the good stuff. See ya, he says, and dissolves into the frosty air.

# ACKNOWLEDGMENTS

My sincere thanks to

- all those who helped this book come into being and endure: *The Erratics'* many fairy godmothers in the world of books, and a godfather or two;

- the people I love and hold in my heart: family and friends who believe in me even when I don't, and my steadfast writer friends;

- Varuna, the Writers' House, in Australia's Blue Mountains—an oasis outside time where writing magic happens;

- and Dr. James Dempsey, Associate Professor in the Faculty of Native Studies at the University of Alberta, Edmonton, for helping me understand Napi. Your generosity touches me.

Vicki Laveau-Harvie was born in Canada, but lived for many years in France before settling in Australia. She has three passports and treasures the unique perspective this quirk of fate affords her. In France she worked as a translator and as a business editor, despite being a specialist in eighteenth-century French literature.

In Sydney she lectured in French Studies at Macquarie University. After retiring, she taught ethics in a primary school. She is passionate about writing, education, and communication.

Her memoir, *The Erratics*, won the 2018 Finch Memoir Prize and the 2019 Stella Prize. It was shortlisted for the 2019 Douglas Stewart Prize for Non-Fiction. She has won prizes for short fiction and poetry.

*A Note on the Type*

This book was set in Garamond, a type named for the famous Parisian type cutter Claude Garamond (ca. 1480–1561). Garamond, a pupil of Geoffroy Tory, based his letter on the types of the Aldine Press in Venice, but he introduced a number of important differences, and it is to him that we owe the letter now known as "old style."

Typeset by Digital Composition, Berryville, Virginia
Printed and bound by Berryville Graphics, Berryville, Virginia
Designed by Maria Carella